WHY JAZZ?

WHY JAZZ?

A CONCISE GUIDE

KEVIN WHITEHEAD

OXFORD
UNIVERSITY PRESS

2011

OXFORD
UNIVERSITY PRESS

Oxford University Press, Inc., publishes works that further
Oxford University's objective of excellence
in research, scholarship, and education.

Oxford   New York
Auckland   Cape Town   Dar es Salaam   Hong Kong   Karachi
Kuala Lumpur   Madrid   Melbourne   Mexico City   Nairobi
New Delhi   Shanghai   Taipei   Toronto

With offices in
Argentina   Austria   Brazil   Chile   Czech Republic   France   Greece
Guatemala   Hungary   Italy   Japan   Poland   Portugal   Singapore
South Korea   Switzerland   Thailand   Turkey   Ukraine   Vietnam

Published by Oxford University Press, Inc.
198 Madison Avenue, New York, New York 10016

www.oup.com

Oxford is a registered trademark of Oxford University Press

Library of Congress Cataloging-in-Publication Data
Whitehead, Kevin.
Why jazz? : a concise guide / by Kevin Whitehead.
p.   cm.
Includes bibliographical references and index.
ISBN 978-0-19-973118-3
1. Jazz—analysis, appreciation. I. Title.
ML3506.W53   2011
781.65—dc22   2010007442

9 8 7 6 5 4 3 2 1

Printed in the United States of America
on acid-free paper

for Irving and Stephanie Stone
in general
and Anne and Dave Tiffany
in particular

Acknowledgments

This book came together during a nomadic year. Jim Macnie and Holly Halvarson offered the perfect country hermitage in which to write it, and while it germinated I happily abused the hospitality of Anne and Dave Tiffany, Jodi Gilbert and Michael Moore, Eric Boeren and Elizabeth Ford, Susanna von Canon, and Hope Carr—not forgetting Elizabeth Tiffany, Reuben Moore, Cecilia and Lucy Boeren, and Misha and Crockett Macnie. It's impossible to thank every colleague whose views inform mine, but in recent years talks with Allan Chase, Dominique Eade, Michael Moore, and Sherrie Tucker have been especially stimulating. I learned a lot from Allan when we collaborated on an abortive book project a few years ago, and he generously vetted this manuscript. Also of help in ways they may not even know about: Bob Blumenthal, Francis Davis, Dorice Elliott, Guus Janssen, Richard Kershenbaum, Art Lange, Lucille Marino, Joe McPhee, Anna Neill, Francesca Patella, Lloyd Sachs, Larry Stanley, Deb Olin Unferth, Karin and Jamie,

Catherine and Indigo, and the Rhode Island Department of Environmental Management. At Oxford University Press, Cybele Tom got this project moving, and Suzanne Ryan and Madelyn Sutton brought it home.

Deep bows to producers Roberta Shorrock and Danny Miller of NPR's Fresh Air, and editors Michael Azerrad and Joe Keyes at eMusic .com, for letting me cover varied jazz topics year in and year out. Some material here began to take shape under their auspices. At the University of Kansas I taught a two-semester jazz history course four years running; thanks to American Studies chairs Norm Yetman, David Katzman, and Cheryl Lester for the privilege, and to many students for their excellent questions.

Contents

WHY JAZZ?

Introduction

Jazz is the topic. Questions?

Why listen to jazz?

It's fun to listen to. Everything else follows from that. Jazz is fascinating as a test of musicians' resourcefulness and as an aspect of African American culture that speaks to people around the globe. But that wouldn't mean so much if it didn't sound good.

Jazz is a world of music in itself, encompassing the joyous dust-ups of dixieland and free jazz, the propulsion of Kansas City swing and breakneck virtuosity of bebop, the loud crunch of electric jazz, postmodern fragmentation, nobility, lust, humor, brains and feet, blues, country, rock 'n' roll. It's all in there.

It's exciting to hear musicians improvise, making a coherent statement in real time, as each player feeds and feeds on what the others are doing. Jazz is also transparent—about processes you can hear, once you're tuned in: themes and variations, call-and-response, contrasting rhythms and feedback loops. This book aims to tune you in if you're new to the music, or tune up your listening if you've already got the bug.

Why Jazz? is a crash course in hearing connections, while answering the kinds of questions new or curious listeners often ask. It's not a guide to the greatest jazz records or musicians, and it doesn't list all the important figures in every style or discuss every phase of a featured artist's career. It's not a musicology book, though there's some light, plain-English discussion of a few technical matters. In the back there's a short glossary of jazz terms, also defined on the fly, but we won't stop to explain what a clarinet or drum stick is.

We'll start with some basics, then take a quick tour of jazz history, zeroing in on a few typical or classic recordings. After that, when you put on a jazz record or go to a nightclub, you'll have a good idea what you're listening to and what to listen for.

Do I have to like it all? Do I need to know the history of jazz to appreciate it?

Many fans respond in a visceral way. They hear something in the beat, in the blend of instruments or in a singer's voice they respond to immediately. For some listeners a single style has everything they need. They may even think it's the only jazz that matters.

But jazz is about variations: how one riff, idea, or style is transformed into another. Seasoned listeners know those *aha* moments, when they recognize some neat or novel sound as a new spin on an old tack. For those payoffs, some historical perspective helps—some sense of the shape of things.

I got into jazz for the sound of it, but the more I heard, the more questions I had about how it worked, how a particular piece fit into a bigger picture: what influenced it and what it influenced.

Jazz is full of allusions. A performance may reference another tune, another version of the same tune, the sound of another performer or genre, or musical practices traceable to Africa or Europe (or Cuba). It's exciting to hear those connections: to hear field hollers and old hymns in Duke Ellington, a homemade West African reed in a John Coltrane blues, operatic arias and brass band music in trumpeter Louis Armstrong's high-note endings.

Do jazz novices need to assemble big record collections?

No. With the waning of the CD, we're now in a post-album era. Most of the individual performances named or discussed are widely available for download. Much jazz is available as streaming audio on the Web—for example, from the invaluable (and long-running) site redhotjazz.com, a searchable jukebox of thousands of early jazz records, and from jazz-on-line.com, which has a good selection of classic swing and bebop. An amazing number of jazz performances shot for films or TV may be found at video-sharing Web sites. The URLs often change, but classic clips of Louis Armstrong, Duke Ellington, Billie Holiday, and many more are usually available for viewing.

Jazz is more than a hundred years old; isn't it old-fashioned?

No, because music with substantial improvised content constantly updates itself. A jazz musician who overhears a pop song on the radio on the way to a gig might paraphrase or quote it on stage an hour later.

Jazz is voracious, ingesting all kinds of nourishment. For decades, improvisers played new Broadway tunes as soon as the ink on the sheet music was dry. Pianist Dave Brubeck heard an odd rhythm in Turkey and made it into a hit. Jazz drummers fused rock and Latin beats into the boogaloo. Jazz musicians play reggae and hip-hop and songs by Radiohead.

One sign jazz still has cachet is that Capitol Records issues the classy adult pop of Norah Jones and Van Morrison under its Blue Note jazz imprint.

Isn't this a short book for such a complicated subject?

Sure. We pack a small bag for a long trip. But there's something to be said for telling the short version. It makes the broad outlines easier to follow.

1
The Basics

What is jazz?

Jazz is too stylistically diverse for any single definition to satisfy everyone. Observers may even disagree about whether certain players are jazz musicians at all.

Still, to get started: jazz is a music of rhythmic contrasts, featuring personalized performance techniques that usually involve improvisation. It mixes aspects of folk and art music, and its aesthetic reveals a strong African American character, no matter who is playing it or where. Jazz is less about what material musicians play than what they do with it: work variations on it by artfully distorting its rhythms, its melody, and even its form.

When did jazz develop?

No one documented its first stirrings, but jazz seems to have emerged around 1900 in New Orleans's black community, evolving out of music already in the air.

How much of a jazz performance is composed, and how much is improvised?

Taking composed to mean music that is totally predetermined, and improvised to mean music created on the spot with no plan in mind, any combination is possible. Duke Ellington wrote a number of pieces in which the solo instruments follow written lines, and improvised content is minimal. "Mood Indigo" (1930) is one example. But even on two versions recorded days apart, Ellington's players vary their interpretation (not unlike classical performers, as far as that goes). Lennie Tristano's admirably coherent "Intuition" was "free improvised"—without predetermined content—by the pianist and four of his musicians in 1949. But having the players enter one at a time was obviously agreed on in advance as a compositional element.

Trying to distinguish between composition and improvisation raises philosophical conundrums. Bebop saxophonist Charlie Parker's compositions sound so much like his improvising, it's safe to say some of his tunes were extemporized melodies that were written down later. Is that improvised or composed music?

Are jazz solos really improvised?

Some more than others. A solo is a foregrounded or spotlighted statement by a particular instrument or musician in the course of an ensemble performance. By tradition in jazz, the content is improvised—an opportunity for musicians to demonstrate their instrumental prowess ("chops") and spontaneous creativity.

In the big bands touring in the 1930s, players might solo on the same tune almost every day, and such statements often became repeatable formulas. When musicians grew tired of hearing a colleague play the same solo every night, they might start singing along.

If a soloist and supporting musicians are attentive to one another, each will influence others' phrasing and accents. But even spontaneous players repeat themselves. They may drop whole phrases they've rehearsed or played before into a solo, consciously (knowing it'll fit) or unconsciously (because it "falls under their fingers").

Jazz musicians are praised for having individual styles, and any recognizable style relies on repetition: of pet licks (phrases they repeat in varied contexts), of certain improvising strategies (like John Coltrane's way of playing rapid successions of scales), or of ways of inflecting a note or shaping one's tone. Does playing the same licks in different contexts betray a compositional or improvisational impulse? Let's say both. Jazz embraces paradoxes, incorporating seemingly antithetical elements: composition and improvisation, order and unpredictability.

Why do jazz reissues include multiple takes of the same tune from the same recording session?

So you can hear how they differ. Even when the routines are set, solos may vary. Comparing alternate takes to a "master"—the version originally released—reveals how much of a solo is actually improvised. Phrases so elegant they sound preconceived—on, say, Charlie Parker's "Parker's Mood" or Miles Davis's "Flamenco Sketches"—may not appear on alternates.

Still, improvisers may keep some ideas in mind from take to take. Tenor saxophonist Coleman Hawkins plays varied solos on four passes at Cozy Cole's 1944 "Father Co-operates," except for a dramatic, climactic sequence too good to discard. Indeed, it resembles the bridge to Hawkins sideman Dizzy Gillespie's "Salt Peanuts," recorded months later, though it's not clear who influenced whom.

What do jazz audiences listen for?

A jazz performance operates on a few levels, which may seem daunting, but that lets you approach the music from several angles. You might focus on the melody instruments, or the way members of the rhythm section (usually piano, bass, and drums) interact, reinforcing or tugging against one another. You might focus on just the bassist or drummer, to hear the many ways they vary their patterns. You can listen moment to moment, as if following a story, or you can think about a bigger picture—how the improvising relates to the written theme, how two consecutive solos complement each other (or don't), how this version of a tune compares with others.

If you recognize the melody, or if it's catchy enough to stick in your mind, you can compare it to soloists' variations. They might, say, play the original tune in a different rhythm, or keep the rhythm but substitute new pitches, or leave the melody behind. Improvised solos may have their own melodic pleasures; Coleman Hawkins's rapturous 1939 "Body and Soul" only hints at the melody as written.

For a particular example, take trumpeter Miles Davis's 1955 "S'posin'," an old pop tune played much faster than usual. (It starts, and builds, on an attractive rising and falling figure that returns three more times.) After a brief introduction by piano, bass, and drums, Davis enters playing the melody, paraphrasing slightly to streamline it. A metal Harmon mute sits inside the horn's bell, to give his playing a more intimate, whispery sound.

The tune as written is 32 bars long. Davis races through it in 30 seconds and then extends it by 2 additional bars, putting off the ending to build suspense. Then the rhythm section suddenly breaks off, and Davis plays 2 more bars, solo, before the rhythm section falls back in. Such "breaks" are a favorite jazz device, a way of generating excitement. This extension-plus-break formula is repeated at the end of every solo here—stretching 32 bars to 36.

After that first break, Davis improvises his trumpet solo as the rhythm section repeats the same form and chords it played under the melody. Every cycle through that form is called a chorus; Davis takes two solo choruses in little more than a minute. Here and there he comes back to the written melody—at the end of each chorus, for instance—and sometimes he plays short phrases that suggest its rhythms or shape. But he also plays original phrases that fit the underlying chords, the way a do-re-mi-fa-so-la-ti-do major scale fits over a do-mi-so major chord.

As Davis solos, pianist Red Garland plays the tune's chords softly behind him, in a clipped, no-time-for-dawdling rhythm. Bassist Paul Chambers mostly plays 4 even beats per bar, weaving his bass line around the notes of the passing chords, creating forward thrust on another level. In jazz parlance that style is called "walking bass." The bass line provides basic orientation to the chords and direction; focusing on it lets you hear when the chords are headed back home. Drummer Philly Joe Jones also keeps the beat. He'd been using sticks on hi-hat during the melody statement, shifting that beat to shimmering ride cymbal under Davis's solo, for a more open pulse. His punctuating accents on snare or bass drum comment on and spur on the trumpet.

One of the miracles of jazz is that piano, bass, and drums, playing in the cracks between each other's parts and spontaneously varying those parts, somehow sync up to get the propulsive lift known as "swing."

Usually, when a band has two horn players, they play the melody together, but on "S'posin'," tenor saxophonist John Coltrane is silent until he dives in on the 2-bar break that caps Davis's improvisation. (He often made delayed entrances in this band.) Now Coltrane solos, and while his phrasing may resemble Davis's, the sound of his physically larger horn is brawnier, and he ignores the melody to improvise lines that extrapolate from the chords. In response to his boisterous approach, the rhythm section turns up the pressure by getting a little louder and more forceful. Coltrane falls silent again after his improvisation, which is followed by Red Garland's; the pianist keeps playing chords with his left hand, as his right takes a linear solo, rather like another horn. After that, Davis returns for two final solo choruses, playing riffy phrases, more rhythmic and repetitious than before. He heads back toward the melody to wind up, and the rhythm section slows for an apply-the-brakes ending.

That gives you some idea of the myriad processes that jazz listeners tune in on. This example doesn't cover all cases by any means, but it's a start. At the end of the solos they might have, but didn't, engage in a round of improvised "trades"—a rapid sequence in which each player gets a few bars (4 or 2, say—or 4 and then 2) to make a concise comment, often picking up where the last player left off: a sort of musical roundtable.

In jazz, what is a horn?

Any wind instrument: trumpet, saxophone, trombone, flute, oboe, . . .

What is swinging?

Swinging is one of the most alluring and elusive of jazz concepts, easier to hear than define: a headlong but relaxed sense of propulsion, as if the music is skipping down the sidewalk. It often relies on small surges and hesitations, on placing a note or accent just in front of or behind where a metronome or tapping foot would put it. These deliberate irregularities create an irresistible slingshot momentum. On the other hand, Count Basie's bassist Walter Page could place his notes squarely on the beat and swing like crazy.

Jazz musicians possess swing feeling to varying degrees, and some observers invoke Duke Ellington's 1932 song title "It Don't Mean a Thing (If It Ain't Got That Swing)" to dismiss those they find wanting. But by that reductive rule, we'd have to eliminate some of Ellington's own music, such as his spiritual "Come Sunday." Luminaries including pianist Jelly Roll Morton and saxophonist Anthony Braxton have been

dismissed for not being heavy swingers, but their contributions as composers and conceptualizers more than compensate.

What's the relationship between jazz and the blues? What are "blue notes"?

The blues is both a tradition and a form. An African American music developed after the Civil War, the blues adapted the vocal styles of communal work songs, street vendors' cries, and farm workers' field hollers—stylized shouts—to a harmonically simple song form. That form, also called the blues, is a durable and supremely versatile template, the single most common form jazz musicians play and improvise over.

The root form is 12 bars long, with just enough chords (basically C, F, and G in the key of C) to make every stanza or chorus a little harmonic journey, leading the ear away from home and then back again.

The blues also has a distinctive scale that splits the difference between Europe's major and minor scales. Where those scales diverge, at the third and seventh intervals—a C major scale contains the notes E and B, the minor scale E-flat and B-flat—is where the blues scale is most ambiguous, hovering between flat and natural. (The fifth, G in a C scale, may also be flatted.) These slightly flat "blue notes" give blues melodies their distinctive tang and grit.

To approximate those in-between notes not found on a piano keyboard, blues or jazz pianists may sound major and minor thirds simultaneously. Major keys are generally considered optimistic, and minor keys sorrowful. To play both at once reinforces the blues' simultaneous acknowledgment and defiance of hard times. As Jimmy Rushing shouts on Count Basie's "Boogie Woogie" of 1936:

> I may be wrong but I won't be wrong always,
> And I may be wrong but I won't be wrong always,
> You're gonna long for me baby one of these old rainy days.

In vocal blues, the second line of a stanza typically repeats the first; the third line caps the thought: an AAB scheme.

Blues form is so flexible and satisfying that jazz musicians never tire of it, but they may subject it to variations: cutting or expanding a chorus to 8 or 16 bars; inserting other, complicating chords into the sequence; obscuring the neat three-line phrasing; playing notes outside the blues scale. Jazz musicians may also insert a bridge, as in a pop song—a second theme, a little side trip.

Alto saxophonist Charlie Parker's 1948 "Parker's Mood" turns the 12-bar blues into an improvised art song. In his initial chorus, the second line echoes the first, and the third line introduces new material: an echo of an AAB stanza. But there's a wrinkle: he squeezes those three lines into the first half of his first chorus. Parker's second and third improvised choruses, the latter after John Lewis's piano chorus, avoid that neat parallelism, though he echoes some earlier phrases in a less formal way.

Parker begins and exits "Parker's Mood" with a declamatory 2-bar phrase which, like the dramatic opening to his second chorus, is a conceptual echo of a field holler. It's a good example of musical roots resurfacing in a contemporary performance—like grandma's red hair coming back generations later. In 1953, singer King Pleasure set words to the saxophone solo, reconnecting "Parker's Mood" to the vocal origins of the blues.

What material do jazz musicians play?

In every phase and style of jazz, the blues is prime source material. Early jazz bands also played multisection rags from the traditional ragtime repertoire, or similar pieces with several themes, along with some contemporary pop songs. The blues-based multitheme hybrids of African American composer W. C. Handy were also popular, his song "St. Louis Blues" especially.

In the late 1920s, there was a profound shift toward sophisticated new pop songs written for Broadway musicals and, shortly thereafter, also for the movies. These songs' sprightly syncopated rhythms were themselves influenced by jazz, setting up a composers-improvisers feedback loop. The songs of great Broadway and Hollywood tunesmiths—including Jerome Kern, Irving Berlin, George Gershwin, Cole Porter, and the bluesy Harold Arlen—are still an important part of the jazz repertoire. Their rhythmic and harmonic sophistication inspire improvisers' lyricism and pose technical challenges: the chord changes might come quickly, with one or more changes of key along the way. In performance, jazz musicians might further complicate those chord sequences, as they do with the blues.

A typical Broadway-style pop song runs 32 bars in four 8-bar sections. The first "A" sequence is sung or played twice, sometimes with slight variations the second time, followed by a contrasting B section—the "bridge," which might leap to another key and wind its way back home—before a last repeat of the first theme: AABA form.

Some composers of jazz "standards"—works in the common repertoire—come from jazz itself, among them pianists Fats Waller, Duke Ellington, and Hoagy Carmichael. Composers had varying reactions to the liberties that jazz musicians took with their songs. Jerome Kern detested them, but Carmichael adored Louis Armstrong's glorious mangling of his "Star Dust," whose melody had been inspired by Bix Beiderbecke's cornet playing.

Jazz musicians also write pieces to play themselves, but many of those new tunes are based on old ones. Melodies can be copyrighted, but not their underlying chord schemes. So jazz musicians took to writing "contrafacts"—new tunes based on the chords of existing ones, occasionally mixing one song's A section with another's B. The most popular basis for contrafacts is Gershwin's 1930 "I Got Rhythm." Its chord sequence—"rhythm changes" for short—is the most popular in jazz, next to the blues.

One reason why: the song's bridge exploits jazz's beloved "circle of fifths."

What is the "circle of fifths"?

Changing chords by the interval of a fifth—from C to G, say—is vanilla-normal, but if you keep going, you'll circle through all 12 keys—C, G, D, A, E, B, G♭ (G-flat), D♭, A♭, E♭, B♭, F—and back to C, a nice musical exercise over a shifting tonal terrain.

In practice, that sequence usually moves in the opposite direction, as on the bridge to "I Got Rhythm." Almost no tune goes all the way around; the circle is often used for for moving between distantly related keys. The "Rhythm" bridge, for example, leaps from the home

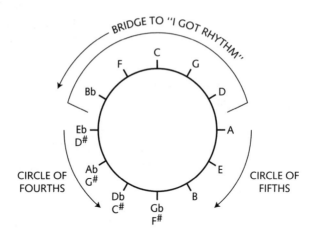

Figure 1. Circle of Fifths. Chords that keep changing by the common interval of a fifth will rotate through all 12 keys, back to their starting point. Chord progressions that move a few "hours" around the clockface nudge improvisers into various keys, to test their skill. Chords may move in either direction. Counterclockwise motion actually results in a circle of fourths, but musicians often refer to it as a circle of fifths anyway.

key of B♭ to D and then winds its way back through G, C, and F to B♭. (If you reverse that sequence, you get the '60s rock anthem "Hey Joe.")

Is jazz about self-expression?

Jazz is only rarely about expressing one's feelings, like Kirk Douglas playing his heart out in the movie *Young Man with a Horn*. Jazz may express yearning or joy or sorrow—or, at least, listeners may perceive such feelings. But musicians are performers, like actors. They may convey a certain emotion without feeling it at the moment.

That said, playing jazz is about making a personal statement—about putting one's stamp on the material. In a way, every improvisation is autobiographical: a portrait of what a player has listened to, what they've worked on technically (or haven't), their tastes, maybe even the region they come from. We speak of Texas tenors and Kansas City swing, though musicians don't need to come from those places to play in that style.

Tenor saxophonist Lester Young used to say a solo should tell a little story. That's an aspiration that jazz musicians take to heart: to improvise a solo with a beginning, middle, and end, expanding on an initial statement, spinning out variations on basic themes, and building and relieving tension as in a narrative. The tale reveals the teller.

Why do jazz musicians play so many notes?

Some improvising is about showing off one's technique, and the joy of playing a fast, accurate line can be infectious. Piano virtuoso Art Tatum's exhilarating up-tempo standards are a relentless onslaught from two hands working together or independently, creating enough subplots for a Russian novel.

A musician's speed and accuracy confirm the endless hours they've spent honing their craft. Of course they can take it too far: everyone's heard guitarists and drummers who don't know when to quit.

Saxophonist John Coltrane was often criticized for playing too many notes, too many scales over a single chord, on solos that might go on for half an hour. But that was less about exhibitionism than searching for new ways to relate scales to chords: his need to fathom all the possibilities. Other improvisers—Count Basie, Thelonious Monk, Miles Davis—value economy. They make a few well-chosen, well-placed notes say more with less.

Why do jazz musicians quote from other songs in a tune or solo?

Some soloists—such as saxophonists Charlie Parker, Dexter Gordon, and Sonny Rollins—are masters of quotation. A shapely quote can add a dash of structure to an improvisation. Or it can be an incongruous joke: saxophonist Johnny Griffin might cap a fast, complicated sequence with "Pop Goes the Weasel." Sometimes the humor is topical: a soldier in khakis enters a nightclub, and a sharp-eyed pianist quotes "You're in the Army Now." Charlie Parker's stock ending, a way of putting his signature to a tune, was a snippet of the song "(In an) English Country Garden."

Dexter Gordon, like Johnny Griffin, is a serial quoter. Soloing on Thelonious Monk's "Rhythm-a-ning" on a 1969 Baltimore concert, Gordon touched on the 1908 pop song "Shine On Harvest Moon," his own jam-session standard "The Chase" (specifically, the phrase in it that invokes the New Orleans standard "High Society"), Rimsky-Korsakov's "Flight of the Bumblebee," the Revolutionary War song "Yankee Doodle," and more—a traipse across the high and low cultures of centuries and continents.

Quotes are intrinsically egalitarian: Beethoven and beer jingles are equally useful. You don't need to be a jazz expert to get the joke. Musicians can overdo it, but there's considerable art to it: the quote has to fit the context of the underlying chords. Certain chord sequences turn up in tune after tune, and quotation capitalizes on those parallels. A quote may even be inadvertent. In the course of improvising a line over a series of chords, musicians may find themselves reinventing an existing song—so they'll finish the phrase, making light of the coincidence.

Quotation was part of the improvisers' arsenal by the 1930s—Louis Armstrong uses it freely on the remarkable "Dinah" and "Tiger Rag" filmed in Denmark in 1933. (You can find these performances online.) Composers did it earlier. The signature *dum-dum-da-dum* phrase from the "funeral march" movement of Chopin's second piano sonata was frequently cited. Jelly Roll Morton's Red Hot Peppers kicked off "Dead Man Blues" with it in 1926; the following year, Duke Ellington ended his "Black and Tan Fantasy" with it, just as singing comedian Bert Williams capped 1920's "Ten Little Bottles."

In America, the practice goes back to the founding of the Republic: James Hewitt's 1798 piano piece *The Battle of Trenton*, patterned on recent European models, is a newsreel for the ears, with bass-note bombs, troops marching in triplets, and snatches of bugle calls, a funeral march, and "Yankee Doodle." The Civil War remake *Battle of Manassas* worked in "Dixie," "The Star Spangled Banner," and fifers' standby "The Girl I Left behind Me." From there the practice spread to songwriters like Stephen Foster. At the turn of the twentieth century, Broadway tunesmiths and composer Charles Ives were habitual quoters; World War I sparked a new wave of quotation songs just as jazz was taking off, such as Irving Berlin's bugle-calling "Oh! How I Hate to Get Up in the Morning." Sampling on hip-hop records carries on this tradition.

Curiously, quotation culture maintains ties to its distant, little-known origins. Improvisers today still quote bugle calls, the Chopin funeral march, and "The Girl I Left behind Me."

Are jazz musicians competitive when they perform?

Sometimes it's for show: good theater. In "cutting contests," where two or three musicians trade solo segments, hoping to demonstrate their superiority and garner applause, combatants may be mutual admirers. That may be why they share a stage in the first place. But these jousts are not always friendly.

In the 1930s, Harlem's Savoy Ballroom had bandstands at either end of the huge room to accommodate two groups, and Chick Webb's house band delighted in trouncing visiting talent. Back then, when bands working out of Kansas City, Oklahoma, and Texas crossed paths on tour, they'd stage their own showdowns—like latter-day hip-hop deejay battles in the Bronx. Winning was good publicity.

According to one oft-told tale, in 1933, when New York's Coleman Hawkins was king of the tenor sax, he got drawn into a jam session in Kansas City with hometown hero Lester Young and others. It's said that the battle went on for hours, exhausting several pianists. One of them, Mary Lou Williams, claimed Young was the clear victor—but then, she was already in his corner.

Cornetist Rex Stewart told of Hawkins, sitting in 1939 at a club where Young and Billie Holiday were performing, and other saxophonists gathered, tearing off a blistering solo at a fearsome tempo. Nobody challenged him that night.

Is jazz America's only true art form?

It's certainly one indigenous American art form. But there are others, about which similar claims are made: bluegrass and country music, the hard-boiled detective novel, the movie Western, the TV sitcom. . . .

2

Jazz from Its Origins to 1940: Roots, Early Jazz, the Swing Era

Is it true that jazz marries African rhythm and European harmony?

There's no single African or European culture, of course, but some generalizing can be useful. Historically, African musicians were pioneers in the field of complex rhythms, while Europeans took the lead in developing harmony: the manipulation of chords (any combination of three or more notes which, when sounded together, Western listeners hear as one complex sound). Jazz draws heavily on both heritages, but boundaries blur. African-rooted rhythms have been Europeanized, and European harmonies have been influenced by African American blues.

Could this mix of African and European elements have happened only in America?

No. They've been mixing for millennia. Africa and Europe are only eight miles apart at the Straits of Gibraltar between Morocco and

Spain, and they were influencing each other's musics long before Columbus. Cross-cultural traffic was especially intense after 711 A.D., when North Africans invaded Spain, establishing a greater or lesser Islamic presence there for almost eight hundred years.

In Spain before 1100, enslaved black Africans, as part of a North African reinvasion force, used drum signals to communicate orders on chaotic battlefields. Crusaders soon heard similar military drum codes in the Middle East. In time, European armies picked up on the idea, using drums and bugles or trumpets to play battlefield signals. Signal corps gave rise to military bands, heavy with trumpets and drums, which in turn spawned nineteenth-century concert bands, which influenced early jazz that sprouted up in New Orleans. That's a long line of development, spanning an ocean and many centuries.

What essential qualities does jazz get from African music?

Jazz has deep roots in two areas of West Africa, from which enslaved Americans were drawn: the savannah/grasslands just below the Sahara desert, and the Congo basin rainforest hundreds of miles south. We don't know exactly what West African music sounded like during the slave trade. But we can extrapolate from knowledge of twentieth-century African and early African American musics.

The rainforest is home to polyrhythmic percussion orchestras of tuned hollow logs—drum choirs. Long complex rhythm patterns are layered over each other, a meshwork of converging and diverging accents. This influence is easy to spot in Cuban music, and but it's also behind the jazz rhythm section, in which a pianist, bassist, and drummer all deal with the underlying beat in their own (albeit more spontaneous) ways.

Savannah music, influenced by Islamic North Africa, is more apt to be about one complicated rhythm at a time, bumpier than a straight 1 2 3 4. Stringed instruments are common; players get a scratchy sound and tinker with pitch, playing flat or sharp for expressive effect.

Throughout Africa, musicians love complex timbres: if a drum sounds too clean, they'll stick a few dried peas inside of it to rattle around. West African melodies generally revolve around pentatonic scales—the five-note series found on a piano's black keys—or at least what ears saturated with European harmony round off into pentatonic scales. Call-and-response is the bedrock of musical organization: one voice shouts, many answer. It's also common in European music and religious services, where it's called antiphony.

You can hear all that in jazz, blues, and spirituals. Call-and-response is everywhere: Bessie Smith sings a line, and a trombone answers; a trumpet plays a written phrase, and saxes respond with an amen; a solo saxophone is prodded by riffing horns; one soloist picks up where the last leaves off; a pianist slides into a Latin rhythm, and bass and drums follow suit.

You can hear complex "dirty" timbres in the roughed-up personalized sound that jazz musicians get on European instruments—in Stuff Smith's raspy violin, the Ellington orchestra's growling brass, the distorted sound of Charlie Christian's or John McLaughlin's electric guitar and trumpeter Miles Davis's fragile cracked tones.

What does jazz get from Europe?

The instrumentarium—brass, reeds, piano, strings—comes mostly from European music. Americans adopted Europe's short rhythm cycles: bars of 2, 4, or 8 beats, and song forms organized in multiples of four—8-, 12-, 16-, and 32-bar tunes.

Also crucial to jazz is European music's defining glory: a goal-oriented sense of harmony, a codification of complex chords and ways to move between them that developed over centuries. Jazz musicians recapitulated that development from simple to complex chords in a few decades, with Europe's example in their ears.

European and African elements are generally complementary and compatible, owing to millennia of cultural exchanges.

What American musical models gave rise to jazz?

Early American music was beholden to the old worlds: African and European call-and-response traditions gave rise to slavery-era work songs. A leader calls, a massed work gang responds, and strong punctuating downbeats help synchronize their labor. Compositions by Duke Ellington, Charles Mingus, and Nat Adderley that are all called "Work Song" catch their flavor. Their shouting tone came down to jazz through farm workers' field hollers and the impassioned antiphony of African American spirituals.

Plantation slaves might improvise songs about masters' foibles and pretensions, impromptu narratives answered by fixed responses from listeners. When a singer ran out of inspiration, he—they were usually men—would pass the lead to another: a jazzlike string of solos.

By the 1840s, mainstream American entertainment was minstrelsy, stage shows in which whites in blackface parodied black songs and body language in satirical or sentimental sketches. Then African Americans in blackface parodied whites' poorly observed imitations, and so on, in a classic, dizzying feedback loop. Minstrelsy was mostly odious, but some white banjo players and composers studied black music enough to catch some of the intricacies of the real thing. African American music began to go mainstream.

After the Civil War, large concert bands like John Philip Sousa's, which evolved out of military bands, aimed to bridge high and low culture. (Sousa was dubbed the "March King," but concert bands usually played sitting down.) Thousands of amateur brass bands, white and black, performed stripped-down versions of concert band orchestrations, using a cornet, clarinet, and trombone or two. When concert bands waned around 1900, their musicians drifted into dance bands that informed early jazz, taking concert-band practices with them.

The New Orleans front line took its cues from bands like Sousa's, in which cornets played the melody, clarinet (or piccolo) sailed over the top playing arpeggios outlining a tune's harmonies, and harrumphing trombones announced the shift from one chord to the next. And like jazz bands to come, Sousa's had contrasting soloists: plaintive balladeers, and virtuoso cornetists who would end a piece with a solo cadenza rising to triumphant high notes as in an operatic aria. Louis Armstrong would run with that idea.

In the South, loud rural black brass bands played by ear for picnics and dancing. Some of those musicians moved to New Orleans and helped jumpstart jazz there.

Concert bands also helped point the way by performing the new music of ragtime.

What is ragtime?

Classic ragtime was African American classical music, written mostly for piano—although as the music grew in popularity, early in the twentieth century, the label was more broadly applied to popular music influenced by ragtime rhythms. Scott Joplin's "Maple Leaf Rag," published in 1899, set the tone. The forms—contrasting sections modulating between keys—were marchlike, but the timing was off plumb. Ragtime was preoccupied with syncopation—musical activity between counted beats.

What is syncopation?

Think of the way a jazz bassist typically lays down an even 4 beats per bar: 1 2 3 4. Count that out double-speed: 1 *and* 2 *and* 3 *and* 4 *and*. A musical line that moves on the *ands* (the "offbeats"), in contrast to a line that falls on the numbered beats, is syncopated. You can hear the effect clearly on the second theme of "Maple Leaf Rag" in any version. The pianist's left (bass) hand keeps up a steadily pumping, almost

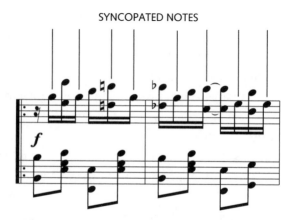

Figure 2. Scott Joplin's "Maple Leaf Rag" (1899), bars 18 and 19: start of the second theme. Even if you don't read music, you can see what's going on here rhythmically, bearing in mind that notes aligned vertically sound simultaneously. Notice the regular, almost marchlike rhythm of the evenly spaced notes for the pianist's left hand on the lower stave, and how various shorter notes for the right hand (top stave) are timed to fall between the notes of the left-hand pattern. Those notes "in the cracks," tugging against the prevailing rhythm, are said to be syncopated.

marchlike pattern, while the right slides between those beats: the *taka-taka-taka-taka* rattle of a steam engine.

A related shift was also going on, from European music's accent on the first and other odd-numbered "strong" beats—1 2 3 4—to the even numbered "weak" beats, or backbeats: 1 2 3 4.

In practice, syncopated lines or rhythm patterns are often more flexible, hopping among the numbered beats and the *and* beats. In the Americas, a key syncopated rhythm is Cuba's *habañera*, a 4-beat pattern with a slightly delayed second beat, the basis for the tango, New Orleans and Chicago blues mambos, and booting rock 'n' roll sax riffs. In jazz and elsewhere, musicians also place accents in the cracks between 1 and *and*. On that 16th-note level, these micro-sub-divisions of the beat lead us closer to the even finer gradations of swing.

Ragtime has democratic overtones, giving power to beats long denied an organized voice. Even before composers got hold of it, "rag-ging" had been a people's art, a folk musician's stunt. Later, hundreds of amateur home pianists, mostly women, wrote their own rags after learning ragged timing from sheet music.

Composers worked out intricate variations. In the "secondary rag" syncopation, over a 2/4 beat, even 16-to-the-bar 16th notes are grouped in threes. Those three-note units repeat four times every three bars, for an out-of-sync effect like wheel spokes appearing to rotate backwards on film. The three-note riffs of 1914's popular "Twelfth Street Rag" and Glenn Miller's "In the Mood" move to the secondary rag.

The flip side of that 4:3 ratio is the 3:2 triplet: a group of three notes evenly divided over 1 or 2 beats. "Swing triplets" are the same, phrased less evenly. All these 3:2 ratios are stylized representations of West African drum choirs' interlocking superimposed rhythms, and they appear in jazz in many guises.

What was the first jazz record?

By general agreement, the first is said to be "Livery Stable Blues" with "Dixie Jass Band One Step" on the flip side, recorded in New York on February 26, 1917, by the Original Dixieland Jazz Band, a white group from New Orleans. It's pretty good and is the earliest documentation of a typical New Orleans front line, with cornet (the stubby horn soon to be replaced by trumpet) batting out the lead melody, clarinet skating over the top, and trombone sweeping up the rear and sliding up on the next chord. They make liberal use of breaks, pauses in which most of the band breaks off to let a soloist make a brief comment.

But there's a but: the quintet didn't improvise much, or not here at least. That's obvious on "Livery Stable Blues," in which the horns play exactly the same licks every time they cycle through vaudeville-ready barnyard impersonations: serial breaks for cock-a-doodle clarinet, horse-whinny cornet, and moo-cow trombone.

The African Americans from New Orleans touring the vaudeville circuit as the Creole Band might have recorded earlier, but cornetist Freddie Keppard is said to have balked at the money or feared that records would make it easier for other bands to rip them off.

Still, jazz wasn't created in a single burst of inspiration; it evolved on several fronts. Three African American takes on Wilbur Sweatman's secondary-ragging "Down Home Rag" catch jazz emerging from late ragtime, before the Original Dixieland Jazz Band.

New York bandleader James Reese Europe's 1913 string orchestra version approaches the collective excitement and propulsion of jazz. There's plenty of power riffing from multiple banjos and mandolins as the musicians whoop like cowpokes headed for town. His "Down Home Rag" is almost there.

Early in 1916, vaudeville's Versatile Four cut a miniaturized version of Europe's arrangement, for two banjos, piano, and the drums of the astonishing Charlie Johnson, who used a small set-up centered on snare drum. (The drum set itself—a collection of diverse percussion instruments arrayed before a single player—was a vaudeville innovation.) Johnson is the most swinging instrumentalist on record in the 'teens. His headlong groove and high energy are thoroughly modern, while his rolls and other rudiments expose jazz drumming's roots in military bands. His firm, pushy 2/4 beat is punctuated by offbeat accents on woodblocks and clanging cymbal, and siren blasts on a novelty whistle. Drums fire up the banjos, which paraphrase the repeat-till-you-drop central riff.

On Wilbur Sweatman's own "Down Home Rag," his clarinet is backed by piano, fiddle, and pumping saxophone used as a surrogate bass. Secondary-rag riffing and the tune itself would find their way into country music, and Sweatman's jaunty phrasing points toward country fiddling. He gives us a taste of a jazz soloist's freedom on the back half, varying his line a bit, phrasing still more freely, and leaning into high notes with voicelike inflections. This sounds like jazz, in December 1916, two months before the Original Dixieland Jazz Band debuted.

Oddly, the most relaxed swinger on record then wasn't in jazz, or native to the United States, or even an instrumentalist: black Bahamas-born vaudeville comic and singer Bert Williams. On a 1914 spoof of ragtime, "You Can't Get Away from It," his finely calibrated hesitations and surges serve his comic timing, as his swooping voice and slide trombone goad and imitate each other. Two famous students of Williams's drawled, between-the-lines asides were screen comedian W. C. Fields and peerless jazz humorist Fats Waller.

What is boogie-woogie?

Boogie-woogie is an early manifestation of jazz piano, a rolling, busy blues style spiced with some Cuban syncopations. Jimmy Blythe's 1924

"Chicago Stomp" may be the first on record, but the style had been around in some form since early in the century. It was an improviser's, not a composer's, music, but as in ragtime, pianists' hands have independent roles. The left plays a fast steady bass pattern in 8th notes, often walking up and down a scale—a forerunner of 4/4 walking bass—while the right hand piles on lines in contrasting rhythms.

Self-taught pianists boogied for tips in southern logging camps, pounding on whatever beat-up pianos they found there. They often traveled between camps by passenger or freight train, and the varied click-clack of cars rolling over switches and bridges put polyrhythms in their ears. Fast numbers like Meade Lux Lewis's 1936 "Honky Tonk Train Blues" link those rhythms with West African drum choirs' intricate interlocking patterns.

In the later 1930s, after decades at the margins, working-class boogie-woogie mushroomed into a national craze, infecting pianists groomed in other styles, and unbluesy white pop acts like the Andrew Sisters with their "Boogie Woogie Bugle Boy." The fad had run its course in jazz by the end of World War II, but its influence would spread via country music to rock 'n' roll. It also caught on overseas, a symbol of modernity picked up from American troops in Europe and occupied Japan.

What is stride piano?

This streamlined New York style of the 1910s and '20s was a late phase of ragtime. In classic rags, a pianist's left hand strides back and forth between left and middle keyboard, alternating bass notes and chords from one beat to the next, while the right hand phrases more freely. Stride piano takes off from that left-hand move, but with some startling disruptions; it's the beginning of modern jazz piano, in which the left hand's role is more intermittent and flexible. The blues influence is also stronger than in ragtime.

Stride players were fiercely competitive. They could play fast and improvise in all keys, and they prided themselves on cutting the competition wherever pianists gathered. The big three were James P. Johnson, Willie the Lion Smith, and Fats Waller, who were nonetheless generous with their peers. Johnson mentored Waller; all three encouraged the young Duke Ellington; Waller informally schooled New Jersey's Bill Basie before he got the nickname Count.

Contemporary or later nonspecialists including Earl Hines, Art Tatum, Thelonious Monk, and Jaki Byard sometimes punctuated their solos with bursts of stride piano. By the '60s, stride was considered old-fashioned, but in the postmodern age, younger players such as Marcus Roberts and Jason Moran brought it back.

Why was New Orleans a center for early jazz?

Many cultural influences flowed through the city, which had passed through Spanish and French control. Military bands visited from Cuba before 1800, and Cuba's Congo-derived polyrhythms had greater influence in this Caribbean port than anywhere else in the United States. Before the Civil War, the white New Orleans composer Louis Moreau Gottschalk had brought the syncopated *habañera* rhythm back from Havana, and on Sundays in Congo Square, slaves gathered, preserving West African drumming and dancing traditions. Postwar, trained mixed-race Creole musicians began to mingle with brass band blasters from the countryside. New Orleans had extensive social networks; musicians were always in demand for dances, parades, and funeral processions. All these factors led to the emergence of jazz bands around 1900.

Who was Buddy Bolden? Did early New Orleans jazz get recorded?

Cornetist and bandleader Buddy Bolden was jazz's original doomed hero; mental illness had taken him off the scene by 1907. He didn't record, but musicians later swore to the earthy power of his blues and to a huge sound that carried over improbable distances.

There were no recording studios in New Orleans, and its musicians began making records only after moving north as part of the Great Migration of African Americans from the rural south to such cities as Chicago. Jelly Roll Morton and the great New Orleans cornetists Joe "King" Oliver and Louis Armstrong all started recording in 1923, while based in Chicago. No one knows for sure what the first jazz sounded like.

Do recordings give an accurate picture of early jazz bands?

No. The technology was primitive, and some instruments were considered unrecordable, such as string bass, which, when plucked, had a deep, percussive, and quick-fading sound that was perfect for jazz rhythm. Charlie Johnson's 1916 recordings notwithstanding, drum kits were also deemed problematic; percussionists were mostly limited to clip-clop woodblocks and quickly choked cymbals. In 1946, for the album *Talking and Drum Solos*, drummer Baby Dodds demonstrated how he'd played live with Oliver and Armstrong in 1923. His busy, pulsating work rife with military rudiments is startlingly unlike what he got to do on early records.

To make up for the loss of drums' percussive snap in the studio, a band's guitarist or bassist might instead play banjo, either briskly strummed or picked in approximation of a bass part.

Musicians would stretch out live, but discs could accommodate only three minutes of music, so the improvising was curtailed. That and poor sound quality can make early jazz records frustrating for modern listeners.

Even so, King Oliver's "Dippermouth Blues," from his first April 1923 session, packed in six improvised blues choruses: two by clarinetist

Johnny Dodds, one by Louis Armstrong (making his debut, at 21), and the last three by Oliver himself. He shapes the notes coming out of his cornet's bell using a mute, for voicelike "wah-wah" inflections akin to a blues harmonica player's. (Oliver's pianist, by the way, was Lil Hardin, who soon would marry Armstrong.)

While Oliver's recordings imperfectly rendered the sound of his live septet, pianist Lovie Austin, another early jazzwoman, used just cornet and clarinet, instruments that recorded well, on 1924's "Traveling Blues." She'd already been using the same trio to back classic blues singers such as Ida Cox and Ma Rainey.

What is classic blues?

Classic blues was the one jazz or blues field totally ruled by women, the best of them emotive, powerful shouters like the great Ma Rainey and the even greater Bessie Smith, who had the most arresting voice on record. On the 1927 flood disaster song "Back Water Blues," with James P. Johnson on piano, Smith comes on like a force of nature.

The style flourished on tent show and vaudeville circuits starting in the 1910s, and on record in the '20s. On record, a singer was backed by piano and usually a horn or two that interacted with her in classic call-and-response. At the end of every sung line, a horn would interject commentary that could be sympathetic, mocking, or both. That could make for a complex emotional tone: the band hoots as the singer sobs. The crying derisive answerbacks on Rainey's 1925 "Bessemer Bound Blues" are by cornetist Joe Smith and trombonist Charlie Green from Fletcher Henderson's band, using plumbers' rubber plungers as wah-wah mutes.

Accompanying Rainey or Bessie Smith on record was an education for jazz musicians and helped wean New York horn players off outmoded ragtime rhythms in favor of explicitly bluesy and voicelike playing. The sweetness of Joe Smith's accompaniment on Rainey's "Chain Gang Blues" suggests why Bessie Smith was said to prefer him to Louis Armstrong. On Smith's "I Ain't Gonna Play No Second Fiddle," Armstrong sounds a little more in it for himself, providing competitive subtext.

Armstrong is more restrained elsewhere, as on Smith's 1925 "St. Louis Blues" where harmonium in place of piano adds a dash of church feeling, decades before Ray Charles's gospel-blues hybrids. The connection between spirituals and heartfelt classic blues was plain to many of her listeners. Bessie's repertoire wasn't entirely blues—she did some pop songs in the same thundering, emotional style.

Why do jazz people go on so about Louis Armstrong?

He influenced everybody. Of all 1920s jazz soloists, he had the surest grasp of the subtleties and refinements of swing. The shift from New Orleans–style collective horn playing to jazz as a soloist's music is mostly because of him: he needed elbow room to express himself unencumbered. Armstrong's records with his mid-'20s Hot Fives and Hot Sevens are studded with powerful improvisations that make worthy comrades sound feeble by comparison—like clarinetist Johnny Dodds, sandwiched between two unforgettable Armstrong solos on 1927's "Potato Head Blues."

The only '20s Armstrong record on which he leaves no one in his dust is "Weather Bird" (1928), a duet with Earl Hines, a two-fisted virtuoso quaintly said to play "trumpet-style" piano because his punchy right hand was Armstrong-inspired. But everyone bore Armstrong's stamp, from Western-swing steel guitarists to crooner Bing Crosby. The first great jazz vocalist outside classic blues, Armstrong sang with the same creativity and free phrasing he exhibited on cornet, and he popularized "scat singing"—rhythmic vocalizing on nonsense sylla-bles. (He's known to fans around the world as Satchmo, but his hipper nickname was Pops—the name he called everybody else.)

When he switched from cornet to the brighter-sounding trumpet, around 1927, most cornetists followed. His brilliant tone and stun-ning high note work, usually reserved for spectacular ending sequences, demonstrated new possibilities for trumpet players and all improvisers.

Later in life Armstrong would amuse himself by assembling paper collages, but he already showed collagist's instincts on the 1927 blues "I'm Not Rough." It is very rough, from Lil Hardin Armstrong's stomping piano introduction, through a New Orleans collective laced with the mandolin-speed double picking of guest guitarist Lonnie Johnson. (His presence makes this nominal Hot Five a sex-tet.) The band then falls away for Johnson's stinging, string-bending solo, with only faintly strummed banjo in support. When Armstrong joins them to sing a chorus, we're in the realm of voice-and-guitar country blues, a genre that was then just starting to get recorded. But nothing prepares us for the final 16 seconds, when the band expertly mimics the sound of a skipping record—a *trompe l'oreille* worthy of a French surrealist, a practical joke on listeners who'd get up to fix it, and a sly comment on the glitches inherent in reproduc-tive technology.

What's important about Bix Beiderbecke?

Jazz loves a doomed genius. A self-taught musician from an uncompre-hending Iowa family who drank himself to death at 28, Beiderbecke became a potent mythological figure. His life loosely inspired Dorothy Baker's 1938 novel *Young Man with a Horn* and (even more loosely) the 1950 film version.

As cornet player, his gifts complemented Armstrong's: Beider-becke's rhythms were less daring, but his choice of pitches could be more so, informed by French impressionist music. The colorful harmonies in his piano composition "In a Mist" underscore the connection. Beiderbecke showed how white (or any) musicians could profitably draw on jazz's European heritage. He paved the way for introspective trumpeters such as Miles Davis and Chet Baker and the cool jazz movement of the late '40s and '50s.

Beiderbecke's bell-like tone inspired extravagant praise. Guitarist Eddie Condon quipped, "The sound came out like a girl saying yes."[1] On the landmark "Singin' the Blues" with saxophonist Frank Trumbauer's octet in 1927, Beiderbecke's declarative, staccato phrasing and a sudden rapid run paying off with a ripping high note declare his debt to Armstrong. But his softer tone set him apart, and he'd linger over odd notes that Armstrong might hit only in passing. His lines were more wistful and ethereal, less tethered to the underlying chords—more dreamily romantic.

Some depict him as Armstrong's equal, but in truth his influence, profound as it is, has been nowhere near as extensive.

And why is Jelly Roll Morton so important?

The New Orleans–born braggart was an easy target for fellow musicians' mockery, but Morton was a trend-setting pianist, smart orchestrator, and a valuable historian of early jazz. His infamous boasting was at least partly shtick: early jazz pianists always tried to psych out their rivals.

In 1923, after years crisscrossing North America, he settled in Chicago and began documenting his extensive book of compositions, with a series of solo piano recordings uncommonly confident for the time. The swung, limbered-up ragtime of "Grandpa's Spells" and a 2-beat

Whiteman's music was in the air when Fletcher Henderson's seminal African American big band got running in 1924—about ten pieces at first. Its main arranger, Don Redman, seized on how divided horn sections lent themselves to the push and pull of classic African American call-and-response.

On a Redman or Henderson arrangement, massed trumpets, trombones, and saxes might alternately take the lead, or chase each other, or engage in three-way conversation. (An arrangement is an orchestration for a particular lineup of instruments or players, written by an arranger.) A trumpet, trombone, or reed section might include anywhere from two to six players. Sections would rehearse separately to perfect their blend, matching their vibrato and breath pauses. Redman also used familiar small-group techniques like solos, breaks, and stop-time rhythm: the pulsing motion of sharp ensemble accents separated by short silences.

For Henderson's 1925 "T.N.T.," Redman revised an already complex arrangement by its composer Elmer Schoebel. It crams all manner of call-and-response relationships into three minutes: a section answered by the full band; cornet answered by a trio of clarinets (one of Redman's pet combinations, almost a signature); the band answered by crashing cymbal accents; and dialogues for clarinet trio and brass section.

Henderson had some of the best players around, including the four soloists on "T.N.T."—saxophonist Coleman Hawkins; cornetists Joe Smith and Louis Armstrong (temporarily in from Chicago); and trombonist Charlie Green, one of Bessie Smith's frequent accompanists. When Armstrong had arrived late in 1924, the band's rhythms were stiff as a starched collar. Only after he departed a year later did his smoother, more propulsive phrasing really take root.

His influence is plain on Henderson's/Redman's "The Stampede" (1926), in which massed horns charge ahead more smoothly.

march on "The Pearls" expose his roots; on the futuristic blues "New Orleans Joys," he clunks on adjacent keys decades before Thelonious Monk. Like contemporary classical composers Charles Ives and Henry Cowell, Morton was fond of clusters (dense clouds of adjacent pitches) and knew the piano made a good noisemaker or counterfeit drum. His piano sketched the sound of a band; on "Tiger Rag" he'd use his forearm for slide-trombone effects.

By 1926, when he began making a long series of very well recorded sides for Victor, the old New Orleans style was becoming obsolete. But Morton made stunning use of old-school devices: breaks, jostling horns, and multisection tunes mixing social dances, hymns, and marches. In three minutes he might recombine seven instruments seven ways ("Grandpa's Spells," reconceived), play a New Orleans funeral for laughs ("Dead Man Blues"), make the band sound airborne ("Black Bottom Stomp"), or indulge in lowbrow humor ("Sidewalk Blues").

Morton had always been a keen observer of piano styles, of soloist's ideas an orchestrator might use, and of other pianists' strengths and weaknesses. That made him a valuable witness to early jazz. The eight hours of recordings he made for folklorist Alan Lomax at the Library of Congress in 1938 were oral history with piano accompaniment, in which Morton reconstructs aspects of those early days from memory. In one illuminating set piece, he demonstrated how the raucous New Orleans standard "Tiger Rag" was adapted from prim French social dances.

Who was the first great jazz saxophonist?

Clarinet was the reed instrument of choice in early jazz bands; its high soaring role was adapted from brass band piccolos. Before 1920 saxophones were more often heard in variety and minstrel shows; the vaudeville sax choir Six Brown Brothers recorded "Down Home Rag" in 1915.

In 1919, New Orleans clarinetist Sidney Bechet bought a soprano sax, fatter and louder than the woody clarinet but with a similar range. Bechet played it in the fluid piccolo/clarinet tradition, but with the first-among-equals authority appropriate to an instrument made of brass, like a trumpet. His signature was a quick, pulsating tremolo (rapid fluctuations in air flow and pitch), an electrifying sound.

Bechet was the rare early horn player strong enough to challenge Louis Armstrong. They battle for the lead on a rare match-up, 1924's "Cake-Walking Babies From Home" by the ad hoc Red Onion Jazz Babies, with pianist Lil Hardin Armstrong and singer Alberta Hunter. Bechet plays rings around Armstrong's cornet in thrilling collective improvisations. But Bechet spent much of the 1920s in Europe, and he recorded little during that decade.

The first great tenor saxophonist, Coleman Hawkins, played in a corny, popping novelty style on his earliest recordings. Only after Armstrong passed through Fletcher Henderson's orchestra in 1924 and '25 did band mate Hawkins start modernizing. Bix Beiderbecke's musical partner Frank Trumbauer, on C-melody saxophone (sized between alto and tenor), had a more legato approach in the mid-'20s; he could get syrupy, but his smooth lines caught the ear of Hawk's future rival Lester Young.

Bud Freeman of the so-called Austin High Gang—a gaggle of young white players from suburban Chicago who idolized Armstrong and King Oliver—adapted clarinet's squiggly fluency to the larger tenor sax in the late 1920s. His 1933 showcase "The Eel" documents an alternative to Hawkins's tenor style before Lester Young began recording.

Did black and white musicians play together early on?

The United States was thoroughly segregated in the early twentieth century, but musicians occasionally broke the color line—an inevitable development as whites embraced African American music. New Orleans Creole clarinetist Achille Baquet, passing for white, recorded with pianist and future showbiz institution Jimmy Durante's so-called Original New Orleans Jazz Band in 1918. In 1923 Jelly Roll Morton guested on record with Chicago's New Orleans Rhythm Kings, perhaps the most rhythmically adept early white band.

Lonnie Johnson and Eddie Lang recorded guitar duets in 1929, Lang billed as "Blind Willie Dunn" for the blues market. White guitarist Eddie Condon recorded with Fats Waller, Louis Armstrong, and Coleman Hawkins on separate sessions that year.

By the mid-'30s, race mixing on records was common. Benny Goodman's integrated small groups made concert appearances, moving mixed bands into the public sphere. But acceptance came slowly. Billie Holiday, for example, suffered numerous indignities while touring with Artie Shaw's white big band in 1938.

How did the jazz big band develop? Who is Paul Whiteman? Fletcher Henderson?

Early-twentieth-century dance bands sometimes deployed their trumpet, trombone, and reed sections as self-contained entities, an idea taken from nineteenth-century concert bands. (For instance, you can hear separate sections clearly toward the end of Sousa's "Stars and Stripes Forever.") New York bandleader Paul Whiteman applied this principle to syncopated music, as on his 1922 version of the toddling pop tune "Chicago," surprisingly limber for the time.

Whiteman would later hire Bix Beiderbecke, Frank Trumbauer, trombonist Jack Teagarden, guitarist Eddie Lang, and other leading white musicians. He'd probably get more credit now if his band hadn't been so big, slick, and (often) corny; if his star soloists had been given more to do; and if he hadn't been a white man named Whiteman billed as "King of Jazz" in the age of Louis Armstrong.

A hair-raising clarinet-trio chorus aside, the routines are less elaborate to give improvised soloists more room to run. "Stampede" features Joe Smith and—first and last—new cornetist Rex Stewart. Their deft timing shows what they got from Armstrong, but they don't really sound like him; rather, he helped them define their own styles.

In time Henderson's band also developed so-called head arrangements, created collectively in rehearsal, with input from the players. As a sort of flip side to that concept, some arrangers started writing quasi-improvised passages, usually for saxophones, called "soli," as on Benny Carter's "Symphony in Riffs" and Duke Ellington's "Daybreak Express."

The Redman-Henderson style of sectional writing would become the model for 1930s big bands when Benny Goodman hired Henderson to arrange for his orchestra. Henderson also inspired another groundbreaking New York bandleader of the '20s who was even more skillful at placing striking soloists in orchestral contexts: Duke Ellington.

Why is Duke Ellington revered?

Ellington's contribution is too vast to summarize here. He was many people: a percussive, economical pianist; composer of show tunes, ballads, blues and spirituals for orchestras and small groups; bandleader; and diplomat who would tour the world for the State Department in the 1960s. His elegant music and dignified bearing bespoke confidence in the richness of African American culture. One should generally be leery of ranking artists, but Ellington was the greatest of jazz big-band leaders and orchestral composers, thanks to the collective band style he developed with his musicians. (He's always "Duke," by the way, not "the Duke.")

Ellington's compositional style began to take shape in the mid-1920s in collaboration with trumpeter Bubber Miley. Like King Oliver and others, Miley used a rubber plunger as a wah-wah mute, but he tucked a second "pixie" mute inside the bell for a more distant, nasal, sometimes growling "ya ya" sound, like a voice heard over a telephone. Trombonist Joe Nanton picked up on that double-mute technique, and Duke began incorporating their growls into instant classics like "Black and Tan Fantasy" and "The Mooche," a stylized blues tune just as Miley's talking trumpet is stylized blues singing. This growl-oriented material was referred to as Ellington's "jungle style," but it's a stylized jungle out of an Henri Rousseau painting.

Ellington and Miley's "Black and Tan Fantasy" was a breakthrough, a patchwork of original and cobbled-together bits that had its own accumulative power. The opening blues theme paraphrases the refrain of the apocalyptic hymn "The Holy City"—a tune Miley knew from childhood and an allusion most listeners would miss. But the *dum-dum-da-dum* rhythm in the third phrase foreshadows the celebrated quotation from Chopin's "Funeral March" that ends the piece. The second theme, for Otto Hardwick's alto saxophone, is played twice. Its best feature is a slinky, downward-sliding ending. Ellington recorded "Black and Tan" three times for different labels in 1927, and between the first version in April and the remake for Victor in October, the tempo quickened. The second theme sounds markedly better when speeded up. It's a good example of how the right tempo is crucial to a jazz performance.

Also on that October version Miley's two-chorus blues solo starts on a high B-flat (the key note) held for four suspenseful bars before he plunges (and plungers) into a complex solo spiced with blue thirds and sevenths, and even (at the top of his second chorus, around 1:22) a pleading flatted fifth—not that you need to know all that to appreciate his supple rhythms, shapely phrases, earthy growls, wah-wahs, and bent notes. Miley found a way to make a trumpet sing the blues that didn't compete with Louis Armstrong. Ellington's anticlimactic piano solo follows, then a plungered blues chorus from Nanton's trombone that sounds like an echo of Miley's except for a braying donkey bit worthy of "Livery Stable Blues" 10 years earlier. Miley returns for the finale. When the tempo slows, and the orchestra gathers to frame the Chopin quote, the effect is like stage curtains being pulled back on a stunning tableau—the presentation of a new, playful art music.

From the '20s on, Ellington kept an ear out for any quirks of phrasing, pet licks or tricks he could grab from soloists to throw back at them as an element of a composition. The searing tone and slithery motion of alto saxophonist Johnny Hodges defined Duke's sound as much as wah-wah brass did. On 1940's "Junior Hop" for septet, the composer bends blues form much the way Hodges bends the notes of the melody. In general Ellington wrote not *for* his players but *from* what they improvised, making them partners in building a collective style.

Did Ellington always write for specific musicians in his band?

Not always. Once a particular musician's sound entered Duke's vocabulary, it lingered even after that player moved on. When Bubber Miley left in 1929, newcomer Cootie Williams took over his role and style. During periods when Johnny Hodges was absent, his replacements wouldn't stray far from his example.

A few understudies took an inherited technique further, and Ellington would capitalize on their refinements, as on 1940's "Concerto for Cootie." Tenor saxophonist Paul Gonsalves joined Duke in 1950 as a disciple of hard-charging forebear Ben Webster, but then developed his own steaming style, twisting small riffs and melodic bits this way and that. Ellington gave him extended solos on many pieces after Gonsalves's marathon solo on "Diminuendo and Crescendo in Blue" at the 1956 Newport festival brought the band renewed attention.

Ellington didn't tailor pieces for every player, but over time a series of them left their marks on his writing and helped shape the orchestra's collective memory with their contributions: Miley's and Nanton's growls, ex-Henderson cornetist Rex Stewart's bends and smears (as on 1938's "Boy Meets Horn"), trumpeter Cat Anderson's tea-kettle high notes, New Orleans clarinetist Barney Bigard's throaty low register, Jimmy Hamilton's soaring clarinet high notes, Harry Carney's mellifluous baritone sax, the melodic thump of Jimmy Blanton's bass, and Sam Woodyard's snare drum rim shots. A latter-day Ellington number might resemble a trick photograph of several generations of players posed side by side.

Ellington has been fairly accused of not sharing writing credit more readily with sidemen or his compositional aide/alter ego after 1939, Billy Strayhorn. But Duke often acknowledged their contributions, produced small-group records for key soloists under their own names, and made Strayhorn's "Take the 'A' Train" his theme song for three decades. His composer's royalties also kept the band on the road during lean times.

Besides which, in any collaborative art, from painting Renaissance chapels to making movies, the person in charge usually gets the credit. But that person creates the conditions under which inspired ideas can come forth.

Was jazz ever really popular music?

Yes, during the swing era of the 1930s, when big bands of roughly 15 instrumentalists, plus a singer or two, were the top radio, ballroom, and concert attractions. The most successful bands were led by whites such as clarinetists Benny Goodman and Artie Shaw. There were dozens of big bands behind them, across the spectrum from "hot" to "sweet"—from jazz to pop—with the very successful Glenn Miller somewhere in the middle. Pop stars including Frank Sinatra and Peggy Lee started out as singers with big bands.

Black swing bands also flourished in this period. Duke Ellington carried on, and the dynamic, athletic singer Cab Calloway led a successful outfit. Count Basie came to prominence, and drummer Chick Webb's orchestra reigned at Harlem's Savoy Ballroom. Louis Armstrong, based in New York in the 1930s, fronted a big band, singing and playing pop songs.

One important development spoke to an aspect of Armstrong's impact. By the '30s everyone was swinging with more élan than in the 1920s, rhythm sections above all. The old 2/4 time, rooted in marches and rags, had gradually given way to a smoother 4/4. It was better for dancing, and swing is, above all, dance music. Ragtime's self-conscious syncopations had been supplanted by more spontaneous adjustments of the beat.

How long did the swing era last? What factors gave rise to and sustained it?

As eras go, it was a blink, less than a decade. Its traditional birthday is August 21, 1935, when Benny Goodman's orchestra, on its first, sometimes difficult national tour, was enthusiastically greeted in Los Angeles by an audience primed by the band's radio broadcasts from New York. The era petered out during World War II, done in by the draft and restrictions on nonmilitary travel. But partisans sometimes talk about the swing era the way certain white Southerners speak of plantation days, as a timeless Arcadia rather than as a system that collapsed soon after it matured.

Swing's rise was attributed to societal factors as well as musical developments. The Depression cut record sales, and radio was becoming the entertainment medium of choice. In the '20s record buyers had a large selection to choose from, but radio had room for only a few stars featured (like Goodman) on nightly broadcasts. At the same time, in a crippled economy, musicians were driven to accept lower wages, making larger bands economically feasible. Their ranks were often filled with musicians who'd played in radio studios. Fan magazines sprang up to hype radio's new, invariably white stars. An established band's featured performers—like Goodman's Harry James and Gene Krupa—might become next year's aggressively promoted bandleaders.

What's significant about Benny Goodman? Gene Krupa? Artie Shaw?

As just noted, Goodman's 1935 breakthrough ushered in the swing era, and his popularity made the section-versus-section style of Fletcher Henderson standard practice for swing bands. Producer and writer John Hammond, one of jazz's most influential nonmusicians, had talked Goodman into hiring Henderson as an arranger. He'd write about a fifth of the band's charts, some recycled from Fletcher's own band.

Goodman had come up in Chicago in the '20s, crossing paths with trombonist Glenn Miller and the Austin High musicians. Goodman had had classical training, and had spent hundreds of hours in recording and radio studios. He ran his big band like a classical conductor and later played classical music as a second career. The orchestra's music, crisp and ideal for dancing, set new standards for ensemble precision. Goodman was a first-rate clarinetist who peppered his runs with growls and blue notes that sometimes sounded a little calculated. He spotlighted a run of star soloists, including trumpeters Bunny Berrigan and Harry James.

Goodman's totemic hit was 1937's nine-minute "Sing, Sing, Sing," which covered both sides of a 78. It's still a staple of film and TV soundtracks, good for dancing and fistfights. Its hook is Gene Krupa's thundering if not especially swinging tom-tom beat, heard solo, in duo with Benny, and with the full band. His pummeling drive and emphasis on the first beat were much imitated. The arena-rock drum solo starts here.

We might fairly hear that infectious tom-tom beat as a stylized representation of and tribute to the poorly understood nature of Native American influences on jazz. That beat was applied to various "Indian-themed" performances later, including many versions of the jazz standby "Cherokee."

Artie Shaw's big-band music was more wide ranging and ambitious than Goodman's, and his clarinet sound was more opulent. He had hits too—including Cole Porter's "Begin the Beguine," with a spry medium dance beat and Shaw's liquidy, pealing clarinet—but he hated playing them every night. Shaw resented his own success; his downer theme song was called "Nightmare." He disliked the glare of public attention, yet he married movie stars Lana Turner and Ava Gardner.

Shaw kept searching for some new approach and was always forming and breaking up bands. Where Goodman broke the color line by hiring African Americans for his small groups, Shaw brought Billie Holiday and singing trumpeter Hot Lips Page into his big bands.

Preoccupied with incorporating strings into a swing orchestra, Shaw sometimes used too few and sometimes too many. But on 1940's "Temptation," nine strings prove loud and supple enough to stand up to the band. Shaw also liked to yoke odd combinations together. He wrote a nine-minute "Concerto for Clarinet" in 1940 with chamber strings, boogie-woogie piano, Krupa-style tom-toms, and a whiff of klezmer clarinet—postmodernism 40 years early.

What's significant about Kansas City swing? Count Basie?

The rise of radio would dilute the effect, but some regional jazz scenes developed distinctive accents and attitudes. Dozens of "territory bands" toured the Midwest from the Dakotas to Texas. Many were based in Kansas City, a politically corrupt party town with a Depression-proof entertainment industry. A typical Kansas City band played the blues with a smoother 4/4 beat than back east. Their head arrangements were apt to be stripped down and frill-free, with horn players cooking up spontaneous background riffs to propel the soloists.

Count Basie's orchestra was assembled from the remnants of two top territory bands—Bennie Moten's from Kansas City and the Oklahoma City Blue Devils—and epitomized the movement. Basie and his tenor saxophone star Lester Young were the quintessential Kansas City swingers, playing fewer notes that swung harder, perfectly placed over the synchronized beat of bassist Walter Page and drummer Jo Jones.

A fine example of Kansas City's fleet less-is-more minimalism is "Boogie Woogie (I May Be Wrong)," by a 1936 Basie quintet plus blues shouter Jimmy Rushing known as Jones-Smith Incorporated. (This is the blues quoted in chap. 1.) There's no real melody on the opening chorus, just an ascending four-note saxophone riff set against Tatti Smith's trumpet pecking at a single note in a syncopated pattern. Basie plays quick piano chords on the trumpet's beats. His accompaniment throughout is shockingly spare by East Coast standards; never mind that he'd been Fats Waller's protégé. Basie had come to the same radical conclusion that Earl Hines had and Thelonious Monk would: a pianist doesn't have to keep something going all the time. By now the two-handed chugging of ragtime was as outmoded as a steam calliope.

After the Basie band moved to New York in 1936, easterners' swinging got more refined, thanks to his orchestra's example—and its own swing got stronger with the addition of more-felt-than-heard rhythm guitarist Freddie Green. Basie's big band kept a small group's lithe momentum.

His blues theme "One O'Clock Jump," first recorded in 1937, epitomizes the Kansas City aesthetic. It's a concatenation of riffs mostly set behind improvising soloists for classic call-and-response: riffing saxes behind brass soloists (trombonist George Hunt and trumpeter Buck Clayton), and brass riffs behind contrasting tenor saxophonists Herschel Evans (up first) and Lester Young, who enters swinging madly on a single note.

"One O'Clock Jump" is a patchwork of borrowed and repurposed materials, typical of oral traditions, and owes a couple of aspects to Waller. It starts with a boogieing piano lick Basie used to identify himself at the start of some tunes—a byline or signature apparently lifted from Waller. (Fats used it to kick off 1927's "Loveless Love," one of the pipe organ solos he recorded at the decommissioned Camden church that Victor used as a studio.) The jump's memorable main riff—its melody, revealed only in the final 35 seconds—is the recycled first line of Waller's song "Six or Seven Times."

Basie's "Taxi War Dance" of 1939 (with that same piano intro) on the chords to the song "Willow Weep for Me" is similarly light on formal melody: it's all about solos, riffs, and momentum. Weeks later Basie cut a version of 1914's "Twelfth Street Rag" where that old secondary-rag rhythm practically levitates, lighter than air. Jazz had come incredibly far in two decades, partly with his help.

Did Lester Young conceive his style as an alternative to Coleman Hawkins?

Hawkins's vibrant, overtone-rich timbre had inspired most leading tenors, like Chu Berry, whose tone was more leathery, and Kansas City's Ben Webster, who had cultivated a breathy, stage-whispered variation on Hawkins's sound. But Young was shaping his distinctive approach to tenor saxophone before he'd ever heard Hawkins play.

The contrast between Hawkins and Young was striking. (The former was nicknamed Hawk, or Bean; Young was Pres, short for President of the Tenor Saxophone.) Hawk improvised from a tune's chords, the more complicated the better. He liked to complicate them further, as on his 1939 version of "Body and Soul," one of the great jazz performances in any idiom—elegant, unhurried, and beautifully paced. He could also play very fast in uncommon keys, making him a deadly foe at jam sessions.

Pres was tortoise to Hawk's hare. His improvised lines were less harmonically complex; they seemed to float over the chords, ambiguously related to them, while Hawkins spelled everything out. Young's lines had more rhythmic variety and unerring drive. He'd honk repeatedly on one note and make it swing by itself, sometimes fingering it different ways for fine gradations of timbre and pitch. His tone was more ghostly than Hawk's, with less vibrato.

Compared to a Hawkins improvisation, Lester Young's two blues choruses on 1936's "Boogie Woogie" have more economy, more space, more repetition—yet his simple, shapely phrases move in a way Hawkins's rhapsodies don't.

Why were there so few women instrumentalists in early jazz?

Women had been active in ragtime as composers and home performers, and jazz pianists Lovie Austin and Lil Hardin Armstrong began recording in Chicago in 1923. But although jazz is an egalitarian art, musicians were not immune to the pervasive sexism of the time. Pretty much any jazz instrument, piano aside, was considered unfeminine. Some male musicians didn't think women were up to the rigors of constant travel, which was horrendous enough for African American men, who had to search doubly hard for accommodations, meals, and even toilets. Never mind that classic blues singers such as Bessie Smith and Ma Rainey had also lived and worked on the road.

Some women played jazz in professional family bands. One was pianist Norma Teagarden (sister of trombonist Jack and trumpeter Charlie), who did get to record; another was saxophonist Irma Young (sister of Lester and drummer Lee), who didn't.

Why is Mary Lou Williams important?

In 1926, Pittsburgh-reared piano prodigy Mary Lou Williams made her first records, at 16, with a vaudeville act she'd been touring with, Jeanette James and Her Synco Jazzers. On "Midnight Stomp," Williams's rollicking solo is way beyond the capabilities of most jazz pianists of the time, rhythmically and technically.

Mary Lou Williams is easily the most important woman instrumentalist and composer in early jazz. She followed her saxophonist husband to Kansas City and eventually into Andy Kirk's 12 Clouds of Joy, becoming the band's main composer and arranger. She cowrote the bluesy ballad "What's Your Story, Morning Glory?" whose melody echoes in the later lament "Black Coffee" and Elvis Presley's "Heartbreak Hotel."

Other musicians appropriated her ideas—unless she somehow documented theirs first. Thelonious Monk's tune "Rhythm-a-ning" takes off from a phrase in a long quasi-improvised sequence on her

1936 "Walkin' and Swingin'" for Andy Kirk. Her boppish 1944 arrangement of "Lady Be Good" turns up, with few alterations, as Coleman Hawkins's "Rifftide" and Monk's "Hackensack." Ellington and Benny Goodman bought some of her charts as well.

Over the long run, Williams was among few early jazz players who repeatedly updated her sound. In the 1960s she wrote religious music mixing bluesy guitar and ethereal harmonized voices, and in the '70s she played concerts demonstrating the whole history of jazz piano—history she'd lived.

Was the swing era only about big bands?

Where many mainstream big bands had a uniform approach, the '30s saw a proliferation of varied smaller groups. Bassist John Kirby had a tight sextet whose whimsical pieces and intricate arrangements paralleled those of novelty composer Raymond Scott, who had his own small band.

Stride pianist Fats Waller had blossomed into the leader of an excellent sextet, Fats Waller and His Rhythm, and into a relaxed and very funny singer. His comic timing and spoken asides owed much to vaudeville's Bert Williams, but Waller catapulted running commentary into the realm of homemade surrealism—as if making records intruded on a rich fantasy life with imaginary playmates. His 1937 "The Joint Is Jumpin'"—words, music, background chatter, and sound effects—so vividly re-creates the Harlem rent parties he came up playing that it makes his later filmed "soundie" version redundant (though it's pretty funny too).

Big band leaders often drew small units from the ranks of their orchestras. Duke Ellington organized a series of combo dates, fronted by his sidemen; their best records show the same ingenuity and attention to detail as his orchestra music. One of his most famous compositions, "Caravan," cowritten with valve trombonist Juan Tizol, debuted on a septet date under clarinetist Barney Bigard's name.

In 1935, Benny Goodman began leading an interracial trio with Gene Krupa on drums and African American pianist Teddy Wilson, a lively combo that became a livelier quartet when Lionel Hampton was added on vibes. Both Wilson and Hampton also led long series of small-group recording dates, mixing black and white musicians drawn from the ranks of Basie's, Ellington's, Goodman's, and other bands, depending on who was available. Wilson's small-group sides helped introduce Billie Holiday, who soon fronted her own small recording units with name soloists.

Small bands were often more experimental. Clarinetist Artie Shaw's 1940 Gramercy Five featured Johnny Guarnieri on bluesy harpsichord. "Vibraphonia" from 1933, by violinist Joe Venuti and His Blue Five, squeezed over a dozen different combinations of instruments into less than three minutes, with Venuti and horn man Jimmy Dorsey playing two or three each—an early if cheeky example of jazz multi-instrumentalism.

Why is Billie Holiday beloved?

Holiday is remembered for her astonishing ability to streamline a melody, partly to fit her narrow vocal range, and for the way she audibly drew on her turbulent life in investing songs with emotion. Though she didn't record many blues, she has often been characterized as a blues singer because of that deep feeling. (Even the name of her ghostwritten 1956 autobiography is *Lady Sings the Blues*.) She was inspired by Bessie Smith's emotional power and the way Louis Armstrong would alter a tune's timing and contours in performance.

Holiday's voice changed strikingly over 25 years of recording. At 21, on the newly minted movie song "The Way You Look Tonight" with a Teddy Wilson septet in 1936, her voice is girlishly light and playful, as Ben Webster blows tenor sax smoke rings behind her. She loved the stimulation a great soloist gave her, Lester Young most of all. And those horn players were inspired by her, creating a voice-instrument feedback loop. By 1939 she was drawing on greater emotional reserves; she catches the loss and longing of "Some Other Spring" and the operatic drama in the anti-lynching protest song "Strange Fruit."

Late in life, ravaged by heroin, after several drug busts and bad husbands, she was world-weary and knew too well the misfortunes of which she sang. On 1958's LP *Lady in Satin*, her voice is a croak but still expressive. "Glad to Be Unhappy," with its half-spoken introductory verse, suggests why the album is visible in the cover photo to Bob Dylan's *Bringing It All Back Home*. She showed him what a singer of limited means can do.

Fans of one end of her career may be suspicious of fans of the other. Those who prefer the early stuff are said to be callow, those who love the last period are ghouls. So split the difference. On "God Bless the Child," "Lover Man," and "Don't Explain," from her terrific middle years of the 1940s, she's more seasoned than her younger self, and her voice and feeling are heavier, but she can still get around.

When did jazz spread outside the United States?

Jazz spread early and quickly. James Reese Europe's late-ragtime World War I military band known as the Hellfighters laid groundwork in France. Sidney Bechet was featured soloist with an orchestra touring Europe in 1919. Paris welcomed many black musicians after the war, Bechet included; jazz fans there were proud of New Orleans's French heritage. In Europe racism was less overt than in the United States, and musicians were treated more like artists than entertainers.

By the early 1920s, Jelly Roll Morton's tours had taken him to Canada and Mexico. There were jazz bands in Australia, and Dutch musicians played it in Java, soon joined by Indonesian and Filipino players. In the mid-'20s, how-to books were being published in England, and a conservatory in Frankfurt offered a jazz course.

In the '30s, French critics started taking the music seriously, after some Stateside colleagues who get less credit. As European musicians got more adept, more Americans came over to play with them. Coleman Hawkins went to Europe for a 1934 tour with an English band and stayed five years. He recorded in the United Kingdom, Holland, France, and Switzerland, and with the one Continental improviser greatly admired in the States, Parisian guitarist Django Reinhardt.

Django combined the swing of Lonnie Johnson and Eddie Lang with the extravagant lyricism and fearless, stinging string attack of his own gypsy traditions. That he had limited use of all but two of the fretting fingers on a fire-damaged left hand made his playing even more amazing. Reinhardt's ringing sound and charging runs impressed early electric guitarists including Charlie Christian, a transitional figure between swing and the bebop of the 1940s.

Jazz 1940–1960: Bebop, Cool, Hard Bop

What was the dixieland revival?

There was never just one way to play jazz. The '20s had room for Bessie Smith, Duke Ellington, and Bix Beiderbecke, the '30s for Benny Goodman, Fats Waller, and Django Reinhardt. But when big swing bands ruled, in the late '30s, such partisans of loose small-group improvising as guitarist Eddie Condon grumbled that jazz had taken a wrong turn toward regimentation. In the '40s Condon targeted bebop for the opposite reason—too way out.

In the 1930s or '40s, Condon's own solo-oriented bands had a raucous air reminiscent of early jazz, but anachronisms abounded: everybody phrased and swung more smoothly than had '20s players still shaking off ragtime, even if they hewed closer to 2-beat than 4-beat rhythms. Condon was a sometimes boorish wit, a rhythm-chord strummer who didn't take solos. But his nightclub bands gave steady work to early tenor saxophonist Bud Freeman and to the very inventive clarinetist Pee Wee Russell, a master of squiggled asides, perilous phrases like a dash up unfinished stairs, and the all-around right wrong note. Russell's art had less to do with clarinetists Johnny Dodds and Benny Goodman than modern visual artists Joan Miró and Stuart Davis. (Russell's own paintings, later, revealed his admiration for Davis.) Pee Wee was a visionary stuck in traditional settings who never made a successful transition to modernism—not even after being nudged to sit in with modern players, or play modern tunes, years later.

"Dixieland" became a catchall term for any style purporting to hark back to the simultaneous horns and ragtime-derived rhythms of early jazz. By 1940, a phalanx of musicians, fans, and critics insisted jazz needed to go back 20 years to get on the true path, and the dixieland revival was born. Some worthy vets benefited, including Sidney Bechet, whose style had hardly changed. The movement's symbol was rediscovered New Orleans cornetist Bunk Johnson, who spuriously claimed to have played with Buddy Bolden and mentored Armstrong (Bunk's nickname obviously fit). His playing was inconsistent, but a slow "Franklin Street Blues" and steadfastly chugging "Sobbin' Blues" from a 1942 session with New Orleans peers are clues to what very early jazz may have sounded like. On clarinet was George Lewis, who kept playing in this vein into the late '60s.

After 1940, jazz spawned more and more substyles. In response, some musicians embraced new possibilities, some stayed their own course, and others defended their own style by attacking alternatives. So it's gone ever since.

What was Duke Ellington's "Blanton-Webster band"?

In 1940, Ellington's orchestra was at a creative peak. Duke finally added a great tenor saxophonist to his palette of soloists: Kansas City's Ben

Webster, who'd found his own alternately gruff and tender voices in Coleman Hawkins's shadow. "Cotton Tail" (on "I Got Rhythm" chords) is Webster's mini-concerto. His solo on the original recording has become part of the composition; other tenors who play the tune traditionally quote from it. But the chases for banked saxes that follow also have Ben's flavor: the writing and his solo style mirror each other.

Ellington's new bassist, Jimmy Blanton, was one of those virtuosi who make everyone rethink what an instrument can do. There were already excellent string bassists; Walter Page's plump on-the-beat notes made Basie's band jump like a jackrabbit, for example. But Blanton made contrabass violin into a solo instrument. That got Duke's immediate attention.

Their duo "Mr. J. B. Blues" showcases Blanton's percussive, ringing pizzicato tone and leaping fingers. It also brings out Ellington's pithy percussive piano and love of funny chords. Like Basie he has roots in busy stride piano, yet his playing is spare, pared back. Blanton's agile bowing makes you hear bass as a singing fiddle, counterpart to the occasional violin of new trumpeter Ray Nance. When Blanton uses a bow you can hear he's not always in tune, but that left something for followers like Charles Mingus to work on. Blanton was in and out of the band in two years, weak from tuberculosis, which claimed the lives of a few musicians of that era, including guitarist Charlie Christian.

Jazz rhythm had come far since the '20s, and Duke had modernized like everyone else. But he didn't abandon his early "jungle" style, mixing it with more modern stuff on his 1940 masterwork "Ko-Ko," spotlighting several soloists in key roles, among them his early trombone growler Tricky Sam Nanton. "Ko-Ko" is an escalating series of seven blues chorus, building in complexity, volume, and excitement. Ellington builds this cathedral on one brick: a propulsive little four-note figure played on baritone sax and tom-toms on the intro: basically, three 8th notes plus a longer, held note. That motif comes back in the shapely figure that valve trombonist Juan Tizol plays as a "call" in the first chorus (answered by riffing, harmonized saxophones), in sax riffs played over the following three choruses (two behind Nanton's plunger-muted trombone), and in the section-by-section shout-outs that alternate with Blanton's walking breaks on chorus six.

On the fourth chorus, following Nanton's solo, Duke's piano commentary is oddly cartoon-like—full of keys-flying-off-the-piano arpeggios—while syncopated brass punches and a rising saxophone figure in the signature rhythm closely paraphrase the first chorus of Basie's "Boogie Woogie." That wouldn't be the first such Ellington borrowing; his 1927 "Creole Love Call" takes off from a clarinet solo on King Oliver's 1923 "Camp Meeting Blues."

But the last chorus of "Ko-Ko" tops all that precedes it, with streaking, dissonant brass and clarinet chords. On that same chorus, three or four saxophones make a unison line sound richly voiced. Yet for all that activity and much more—momentary shifts or sustained leaps into bitonality—"Ko-Ko" sounds remarkably unfussy. Ellington leads your ear on, step by plausible step. And he does it all in 2 minutes and 40 seconds!

The 1940 band's legacy is bounteous, even for Duke: "Jack the Bear," "Conga Brava," "Concerto for Cootie," "Sepia Panorama," and numerous others. Ellington's ambitions kept growing, through his 1943 Carnegie Hall suite *Black, Brown, and Beige*, a panorama of African American musical culture from work songs and spirituals to Latin dances in Harlem, with more recurring rhythm kernels à la "Ko-Ko." Detractors like John Hammond found it too long, too indebted to European concert music—not real jazz. Duke shrugged off the criticism, kept the band going through bad and then better years again, into the early '70s.

Even so, big swing bands were in decline by the end of World War II, replaced by smaller groups speaking the new rhythmic, melodic, and harmonic dialect of bebop.

*Why did bebop sound so radical when it was
new? Did it break with earlier styles? Why is
Charlie Parker so important?*

Bebop or bop was a self-consciously intellectual movement, a challenge to the notion black musicians were primarily entertainers and to prevailing standards of musicianship. It took extraordinary mental and physical discipline. Boppers had to think fast to play fast.

When bebop emerged on record in 1945, musicians and fans either loved or hated its willfully disorienting tendencies. Soloists might sound like they were in the wrong key and had come in on the wrong beat. The melodies were weird and full of clinkers; the fast numbers were way fast, and the ballads very slow. It was avant-garde but would soon become jazz's new orthodoxy.

Bebop had been developing for years, unheard by most jazz listeners. During World War II, most of the shellac used in making records had been diverted to the war effort. And in 1942, to pressure labels into paying royalties into a musicians fund, the American Federation of Musicians declared a ban on new instrumental recordings. It lasted a couple of years, until the labels began to settle with the union one at a time.

The new style came together in New York, developed collectively by like-minded musicians from all over, at jam sessions in Harlem. Oklahoma City's Charlie Christian helped plant the seeds but died of TB before he saw the flowers. He wasn't the first to play electric guitar, but he made it wail.

Hectic tempos and detours into odd keys sharpened the incipient boppers' skills and discouraged older stylists from sitting in and getting in the way. Bebop's roots were partly in Kansas City's riffing jam-session culture of the 1930s, and the streamlined tone and behind-the-beat swing of Lester Young. Kansas City alto saxophonist Charlie Parker had a dry, almost coarse tone, very different from Johnny Hodges's lush sound with Ellington. Parker's nickname was Bird: he sang in flight.

In the 1920s Bix Beiderbecke peppered his lines with unusual notes drawn from European impressionist music's colorful chords, but two decades later Bird and Dizzy Gillespie and company took it much further. They zeroed in on just the weird notes in extended chords like altered 9ths, 11ths, and 13ths. ("Altered" versions of such rich chords are still more dissonant.) And since those extended harmonies might amount to a whole new distant chord stacked on top of the original one, to the uninitiated, boppers could sound like they'd wandered into the wrong key. They'd also jump out of key on purpose—play a phrase in D-flat against a C chord, then maybe bounce it into yet another key. Boppers could hear how it all fit together and hear the humor in it.

Parker and his mates displaced rhythms in a similarly disorienting way: their written or improvised phrases began or ended on weak beats or between beats. Bop drummers Kenny Clarke and Max Roach started placing loud bass drum accents in odd spots: "dropping bombs." Swing drummers had kept time on bass drum, but the new tempos were too fast for that. Clarke transferred his beat to ride cymbal, for a looser, more shimmering, even more propulsive effect, one of the most profound shifts in the history of jazz drumming.

The boppers wrote contrafacts as oblique as their solos: new melodies on the chords of "I Got Rhythm," "How High the Moon," or whatever. Bop pianists inserted new chords between the old ones, and made the original ones more complex, adding odd notes the way soloists did. You could substitute one chord for another that shared a couple of notes with it—replacing, say, a C dominant seventh chord with a G♭ seventh: what musicians call a tritone or flat five substitution. Boppers loved licks that leapt by the especially dissonant interval of a flatted fifth—C to G♭—which cut an octave exactly in half. This was manipulation of European harmony on a very high level.

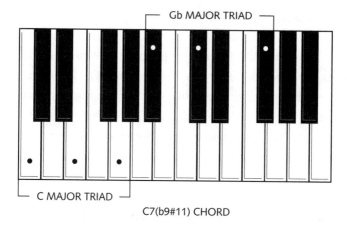

Figure 3. Complex bebop harmonies often combine two simpler chords. Case in point is the dense and dissonant "C7(b9#11)" chord: a simple C triad (three-note chord) with a Gb triad stacked on top of it. The two chords are in unrelated keys, a flatted fifth apart. Such richly conflicting chords may suggest bitonality: music operating in two keys at once.

Those new melodies might begin as improvisations. The Parker vehicle "Ornithology" (credited to Benny Harris) takes off from the beginning of Bird's solo on Jay McShann's "The Jumping Blues." And Bird would insert readymade phrases into fast solos—personal licks, old Kansas City riffs, and quotations from pop tunes or "High Society"—and still sound fresh and spontaneous. His elegance was disarming, could seem almost too effortless. In fact, it often took plenty of effort; Parker was a heroin addict and alcoholic.

Not everyone got him, but many, many younger musicians heard Parker and thought, This is how I want to play. Numerous altoists tried to sound just like him. Charles Mingus later summed up the situation in a song title: "If Charlie Parker Were a Gunslinger, There'd Be a Whole Lot of Dead Copycats."

Like Louis Armstrong in the 1920s, Bird influenced players of other instruments. Quintessential bop pianist Bud Powell's right-hand lines sounded very much like Parker, over punctuating chords and fragmentary bass runs that took off from Earl Hines's and Count Basie's elliptical left hands. Bop trombonists, beginning with J. J. Johnson, adopted a clipped style that avoided broad slide effects; they sounded more like they were playing valve trombone or a lower, oversized trumpet.

What did Dizzy Gillespie contribute?

Parker developed his style by following his ear. In Earl Hines's big band in 1943, he bonded with trumpeter Dizzy Gillespie, who'd arrived at similar ideas from a theoretical perspective while working in big bands like Cab Calloway's. He'd taught himself piano to study complex chords. "Hot Mallets," by a 1939 Lionel Hampton combo, shows off Dizzy's emerging swift and cheeky style. He enters with a quote from Irving Berlin's "Cheek to Cheek," and trades solos with excellent swing saxophonists Benny Carter and Chu Berry. But Dizzy's skittering phrases make them sound like last year's models.

Gillespie and Parker were the classic bebop front line, on record dates starting in 1945, under either's leadership. They played the melodies together—unharmonized, in unison or octaves—with a rough, unfinished edge. Dizzy's tone was more raggedy than his swing idol Roy Eldridge's, more about speed than luster. Gillespie inspired plenty of other trumpeters—some, like Fats Navarro and Clifford Brown, whose technique surpassed even his. But Gillespie was far better known, a natural comedian who looked very striking on stage because his cheeks inflated dramatically when he blew his horn.

Dizzy's second recording of "Salt Peanuts" from May 1945 is an early bop classic, a new line on "I Got Rhythm" chords, with a manic call-and-response head. The response is the tune's leaping-octave hook, to which Dizzy sometimes chants the title, revealing his populist, entertainer's streak. That convoluted melody builds suspense for fleet solos that it makes you wait for, from pianist Al Haig, Bird, and Diz. Swing drummer Sid Catlett catches all the right new accents; he was a fan of Kenny Clarke's, who had been drafted into wartime service. Curly Russell's on-the-beat bass is double-time Walter Page—the Kansas City roots are clear. But even Basie's band sounded stodgy next to this.

What's important about Thelonious Monk?

Monk anchored legendary bop-begetting after-hours jams at Minton's in Harlem, wrote the "52nd Street Theme" that jazz musicians still play to get off stage, and played on a proto-bop 1944 Coleman Hawkins record session. (Hawkins greeted the young mavericks as musicians who could keep up with his own advanced ideas: he'd been using flat five substitutions for years.) But Monk never really sounded like a bopper. He was a master contrarian.

Boppers liked a fleet tone and a squirrelly futuristic line. Monk might break into fast stride piano for a few bars, but favored flat-fingered, almost plodding lines and chords that sounded both dense and undernourished. Monk timed their modern close intervals and clusters to sound like ham-handed gaffes; he was a harmonic genius who played the clod. His comping behind a soloist was a series of unpredictable eruptions and gaping silences. For Monk, a pithy ambiguous chord was as rich with harmonic implications as a Charlie Parker zigzag. He posited an alternative to bop orthodoxy and became a model for later unhurried improvisers and composers such as Steve Lacy and Misha Mengelberg.

Still, like a good bopper, Monk wrote tunes that mirrored the way he played: the composing and improvising were part of the same package. His dozens of memorable tunes include the sublime ballads "'Round

Midnight" and "Crepuscule with Nellie"; "Evidence," whose bridge is punctuated by fiendish offbeat accents; "Misterioso," the blues stripped bare, in which staggered intervals of major and minor sixths walk bowlegged up and down a scale; and "Hornin' In," which doesn't reveal its key for six ambiguous bars.[1]

Monk left a lot of space in his music, yet could be most effective when paired with busy-sounding saxophonists such as John Coltrane and Johnny Griffin in the late '50s. Opposites attract.

Did bebop have impact on the big bands? What about the influence of Cuban music?

Early boppers tried out some of their ideas in a wartime Earl Hines big band, and then a spin-off led by singer Billy Eckstine. Postwar, bop came up as most big bands were fading away; rising wages made them less affordable. Louis Armstrong went back to leading New Orleans–style bands known collectively, if not always accurately, as his "All-Stars"—though one star-studded early edition had Earl Hines, Jack Teagarden, Barney Bigard, and Sid Catlett.

No surviving swing bandleader sounded more energized by the new music than clarinetist Woody Herman. His 1945–'46 First Herd was populated with many younger players, though their first, modern sounding drummer was Dave Tough from Chicago's 1920s Austin High Gang. The band's language mixed old school sparks with bop's serpentine new melodies and fast tempos, as on "Non-Alcoholic," and it sometimes reveled in the friction between old and new. On "Your Father's Mustache" the sneeringly chanted title—a derisive slang term—dismisses both the ostentatiously boppy wrong notes and tiptoeing quote from Stravinsky's *Petrouchka* that precede it.

Dizzy Gillespie led a bop big band off and on, which was most notable for reinjecting Cuban polyrhythms into jazz via collaborations with conga player Chano Pozo like "Manteca," uniting two powerful rhythmic languages. Its main Cuban theme was Pozo's; Dizzy wrote the swinging bridge. The label "Afro-Cuban" was broadly applied to such fusions. But it took awhile for jazz players used to spontaneous swinging to master intricate Cuban rhythmic figures.

Gillespie's interest in Cuban rhythms had been piqued by his Cab Calloway bandmate, altoist Mario Bauzá, one of several émigrés on New York's Latin scene to make occasional inroads into jazz. The first recorded jazz flute solo, on Clarence Williams's 1929 "Have You Ever Felt That Way," was by Cuba's Alberto Socarrás. Starting in 1930, Louis Armstrong and many others recorded "El Manisero," aka "The Peanut Vendor," a Cuban pop song based on a street merchant's cry.

The tune was revived in 1947 by Los Angeles bandleader Stan Kenton. His interest in Caribbean rhythms had been sparked by splitting a bill with Cuban bandleader Machito—who, approaching the jazz-Cuban fusion from the other direction, hired Charlie Parker and other jazz musicians for record dates.

In the late '40s and in the '50s, many big and small jazz bands added conga or bongos for a cosmetic application of Cuban feeling, layering Latin beats over a jazz drummer's swing time.

Were there bebop singers?

One of the very best was a swing convert. Ella Fitzgerald had come up as a teenage prodigy with Chick Webb's big band in the 1930s. On a split tour with Dizzy Gillespie in 1946, she often sat in with his big band and developed a feel for the new idiom. She recorded "Oh, Lady Be Good" and "How High the Moon" as tours de force for her newfound bop chops and fast scat singing. Both tunes became staples of her live shows, where she'd re-create aspects of the records. This sometimes happens to improvisers: they play an impromptu solo when recording a song, and then audiences want to hear it the same way live. So performers memorize their own recorded solos; an improvisation in effect becomes a composition.

Fitzgerald's pyrotechnic scatting was so popular that it obscured her exceptional taste as interpreter of classic pop songs, to which her warm timbre was ideally suited. That imbalance was corrected by her masterful series of *Songbooks* devoted to individual composers such as Gershwin, Porter, Arlen, and Ellington starting in 1956.

Sarah Vaughan had always been a modernist, singing with the bop-incubating Earl Hines and Billy Eckstine bands. A pianist, she had an excellent grasp of harmony. Vaughan recorded "Lover Man" with Gillespie in 1945, a model for slow, lingered-over bop ballads. But her 1954 version is superior; her voice and vibrato are riper, her feeling and nuances deeper, her departures from the melody more artful and subtly blues-tinged. It's one of the great jazz ballads. She was a formidable scat singer too, as on "Shulie a Bop" from the same '54 session.

Bop singers, like bop instrumentalists, were habitual quoters. On "Oh, Lady Be Good," Fitzgerald echoes her own 1938 hit with Chick Webb, "A-Tisket, A-Tasket" and Dizzy's "Oo-Bop-Sh'Bam" among other tunes, and imitates Slam Stewart's way of singing along with his bowed bass. Both Fitzgerald and Vaughan might also sing the lyric when they quote a tune, footnoting their citations.

Why do jazz musicians record with string orchestras?

Mostly because Charlie Parker did, but he wasn't the first. Paul Whiteman added violins to his orchestra in the 1920s, and Artie Shaw integrated strings into some of his swing bands. Strings, and sometimes a few pastel woodwinds, were used to "sweeten" dates by singers like Billie Holiday and Sarah Vaughan by the mid-1940s.

Parker fulfilled a long-standing ambition to record with strings beginning in 1947, when he dropped by a session where arranger Neal Hefti was recording a big band plus strings, and Bird winged an impromptu solo on "Repetition." He made records and live appearances fronting his own string orchestras starting in 1949. On the surface these recordings are strikingly unlike his earlier bebop sides; the tunes are standards, and the charts by hired arrangers are lush to a fault. Parker displays his usual flair for airborne improvisation—though whether because or in spite of his backing is an open question.

Many other jazz soloists followed suit. Hefti wrote string charts on standards for Clifford Brown to play over in 1955; that album's not bad, but in truth most such dates sound like misguided attempts to add a veneer of "class" to jazz.

One of the more successful examples is tenor saxophonist Stan Getz's 1961 album *Focus*, for which arranger Eddie Sauter wrote out the often rhythmically charged orchestral parts but left Getz free to improvise over the top, relying on his consummate lyricism as a soloist. The Sauter-Getz soundtrack to Arthur Penn's 1965 film *Mickey One* is a wilder reprise of the same concept.

Starting in the 1950s, the movement known as "third stream" sought to integrate jazz improvisation and classical forms. Some third-stream pieces deployed strings, such as Gunther Schuller's "Variants on a Theme of Thelonious Monk (Criss Cross)," recorded in 1960 with a mixed classical-jazz ensemble, including saxophonists Ornette Coleman and Eric Dolphy. In 1972, Coleman premiered his own *Skies of America*, a suite for symphony orchestra and his own occasional alto sax. But such works are not usually considered instances of jazz and strings.

How did jazz lay the groundwork for rock 'n' roll? For country music?

Mostly via "jump bands" and rhythm-and-blues. Jump bands aimed for the wallop of Basie's riffing blues, but with a small group. The prototype was Louis Jordan and His Tympany Five, a Harlem attraction that went west during World War II to make soundies, short films for video jukeboxes. Jordan celebrated quotidian pleasures and neighborhood rituals, as on "Beans and Cornbread"—part street-corner rumble, part church service—and "Saturday Night Fish Fry." A song's protagonists and target audience were one, anticipating rock's teen operas. With jump bands, the urban pop of rhythm-and-blues (R&B) starts branching away from jazz.

Los Angeles was prime jump territory, the farthest reach of the blues belt, where black migrants from Texas and elsewhere had settled. Wartime factory jobs generated spending money and places to spend it. Here as elsewhere, tenor saxophonists like Dexter Gordon or Vi Burnside—of the all-women Sweethearts of Rhythm, jazz's Rosie the Riveters—combined Lester Young's booting licks with Coleman Hawkins's beefy sound. On Lionel Hampton's 1942 smash "Flying Home," Los Angeles tenor Illinois Jacquet, who hailed from Texas, rides one note for bars at time. That Lester Young move soon became a staple of catatonic R&B honkers like Big Jay McNeely. By 1947, LA's jumpy Roy Milton and His Solid Senders were playing something very like rock 'n' roll on "Hop Skip and Jump."

Jazz fed rock's country heritage too: the boogie piano, walking bass, fiddle breaks and syncopated guitar rags were all rooted in ragtime, blues, or jazz. In the early '30s, Kansas City swing bands prowled the same territories as Western swing bands like Bob Wills's and Milton Brown's, with their slingshot rhythms, and steel guitarists like Bob Dunn inspired by Louis Armstrong solos. Louis and Lil Armstrong had played on country pioneer Jimmie Rodgers's "Blue Yodel No. 9" in 1930.

Country influenced jazz, too. Texas-reared trombonist Jack Teagarden had honed his minimal-slide technique playing fast fiddle tunes, and his relaxed vocal ballads could put you in mind of a cowboy singing 'round a campfire. Bob Crosby's small band played swing, dixieland, and hillbilly styles. Early electric guitarist Floyd Smith, on "Floyd's Guitar Blues" with Andy Kirk in 1939, played steel (slide) guitar like a Western swinger. That slide technique itself was derived from the blues and Hawaiian music.

What is cool jazz?

Pure bebop is beautiful but severe. The fast tempos were exhausting, and those astringent unison melodies begged to be harmonized, orchestrated. Cool jazz softened up bop, but not in a bad way. Cool evolved on several fronts.

Bop's complex chords sped by in fast sequences. But big-band leader Claude Thornhill and his arranger and disciple Gil Evans loved those chords for their own sake, for the sublime mix of tension and calm when, in a 13th chord, all the notes of a scale sound at once. Thornhill had specialized for years in impressionist chords that hung in the air like clouds; his quiet theme was called "Snowfall." In the late '40s, the bop tunes that Evans arranged for Thornhill took on a different character when voiced by clarinets and cup-muted trumpets. The subtler lighting called attention to the witty reversals in Charlie Parker's "Anthropology."

Jimmy Giuffre's chart for Woody Herman's 1947 "Four Brothers" was in the tradition of "soli" for harmonized saxes, but with closer, cooler voicings. That hit helped establish tenor player Stan Getz, who coupled Lester Young's cool detachment with a lovely tone. Young's way of floating above the chords and the beat went viral after World War II.

New York pianist Lennie Tristano, alto saxophonist Lee Konitz, and tenor Warne Marsh played bop with deep commitment but shunned gratuitous flash: no lurid outbursts. They'd improvise long lucid lines and intertwine in spontaneous counterpoint, a practice out of Bach as well as Bird. Dave Brubeck was working on similar ideas at Mills College in California.

Many of these players converged in 1949. Bird's current trumpeter, Miles Davis, had never felt comfortable playing loud and fast. He and Gil Evans, Dizzy Gillespie's pianist John Lewis, and Gerry Mulligan, a baritone saxophonist with a soft post-Pres sound, began writing tunes and arrangements for a six-horn nonet. It was a miniaturized Thornhill band, fronted by Davis on its rare gigs. Konitz played alto; his Thornhill bandmate Bill Barber was on tuba.

The nonet was a superb vehicle for Davis. The less he hurries, the better he sounds; his cracked notes are as expressive as a blues singer's. The harmonies nod to Thornhill and "Four Brothers," but the arrangers optimize the scaled-down lineup by combining and recombining instruments, not unlike Jelly Roll Morton with his Red Hot Peppers. There are breaks, counter-lines behind melodies, and murmuring background horns. With cool as with bebop, jazz reinvented itself out of its own root materials.

Later the nonet's releases would be collected on *The Birth of the Cool*—part of the big switch in the '50s from two-sided 78s to long-playing LPs.

The cool sound was contagious. It spread to Los Angeles, via East Coast transplants such as Mulligan and Bronx-reared trumpeter Shorty Rogers, whose octet was patterned on Davis's nonet. But his Giants had their own strong voices: gospel-steeped pianist Hampton Hawes; volatile, heartbreaking bop altoist Art Pepper; "Four Brothers" composer Jimmy Giuffre on tenor. Save Hawes, all these players were white. Before long there was a tendency back East to denigrate cool as too sun-bleached and Californian. Never mind that the birth of cool jazz took place in Manhattan.

Shorty Rogers would say later that his real ideal was Basie's airy way with the blues. The trumpeter's start-and-stop riff blues "Martians Go Home" for a 1955 quintet is even more skeletal than Monk's "Misterioso." Pete Jolly's spare piano underscores the Basie connection. Giuffre plays clarinet, on which he gravitated toward warm and woody low notes, very understated. Punctuated by eloquent silences, "Martians Go Home" is about what's not played as much as what is.

West Coasters were good at reducing things. In 1952 Mulligan started a quartet with the California scene's answer to Miles Davis— Chet Baker, a soft-spoken trumpeter and reckless junkie who sang like a choirboy. The quartet had no piano: they already knew what chords to base their solos on, and didn't need a pianist to sound them. To thicken the texture, Mulligan and Baker might play in spontaneous counterpoint, as on "Bernie's Tune." From there it'd be short steps to Ornette Coleman's 1959 two-horn quartet; without piano, why be fastidious about following chord changes at all?

The East had cool schoolers too. Tristano carried on; the Davis nonet's pianist John Lewis founded the Modern Jazz Quartet, self-consciously invoking baroque fugues and counterpoint; George Russell composed intricate works for small groups. There were also black hard bop musicians in Los Angeles, such as saxophonist Harold Land and bassist Curtis Counce.

What is hard bop? Soul jazz?

The 1950s music of hard bop stuck with bebop's two-horn combos, virtuoso improvising and serial solos. But its priorities were different. Like R&B, hard bop featured less complicated chord changes. There were fewer Broadway tunes, more blues, and sometimes self-conscious echoes of the soulful feeling of black churches: gospelly piano chords and "amen" responses from horns. That churchy end of hard bop, sometimes known as "soul jazz," reasserted the music's African American roots as the Civil Rights Movement emerged, and pointedly distinguished it from mostly white cool jazz.

A prime example is Horace Silver's 1955 "The Preacher," a simple down-home melody that proceeds at a carefree medium lope. Drummer Art Blakey accents the backbeats; bassist Doug Watkins plays little fragments of bluesy melody while keeping time. Kenny Dorham plays post-Dizzy trumpet; Hank Mobley slurs on tenor sax with a big tone and some Lester Young–style skidding across the beat. Silver's piano solo is full of riffy repeats and bluesy little figurations from the right hand and terse grunting interjections from the left.

The same quintet also worked as Art Blakey's Jazz Messengers, a band that would mine the hard bop vein into the '90s. Along the way Blakey introduced dozens of star players who'd hone their chops in his employ, including Lee Morgan, Wayne Shorter, Freddie Hubbard, and Wynton Marsalis. Horace Silver kept writing simple, catchy tunes even longer than that.

By contrast, the quintet that drummer Max Roach formed with perhaps the most accomplished post-Gillespie trumpeter, Clifford Brown, lasted only two years. In 1956, Brown died in a road accident while on tour, like Bessie Smith and Chu Berry before him.

More ambitious than Blakey, Roach thought like an orchestrator, looking to vary textures and procedures. The Brown-Roach quintet's 1954 take on Cole Porter's "I Get a Kick Out of You," with its tricky leaps in and out of waltzing 3/8 time, prefigures Roach's deeper explorations of odd meters soon to come. Their version of Bud Powell's "Parisian Thoroughfare" is rife with touristic color—mock car horns, can-can music, a snippet of the French national anthem—that doesn't impede spirited blowing.

Another trend related to hard bop was the rise of jazz organ groups, using the Hammond B-3 portable electric console with its many tone settings for two keyboards, plus bass pedals for a player's roving left foot, and a volume pedal for the right. The B-3, designed for small churches, was by the late '50s a staple of barrooms in urban black neighborhoods. Philadelphians such as Jimmy Smith and Shirley Scott led the way, playing the blues with inevitable churchy overtones, many dramatic swells in volume, and all manner of recombined dense timbres.

How did Charles Mingus's music develop?

In Los Angeles in the postwar 1940s, the precocious composer and bassist had written big-band ballads inspired by Duke Ellington, and his 1947 "Mingus Fingers" with Lionel Hampton's orchestra marked him as a successor to Ellington bass wiz Jimmy Blanton. In New York in the early '50s, Mingus's interest in counterpoint drew him toward Lennie Tristano's cool jazz; Mingus wrote out an intricate, quasi-improvised solo for altoist Lee Konitz, "Extrasensory Perception," recorded at Tristano's studio.

Mingus had been searching for a new direction. Hearing hard bop and soul jazz connect to the feeling of the black church sparked his mature music. In 1955 he started teaching his musicians their parts by ear, singing or playing them on piano instead of handing out sheet music. The vocalized cry his horn players started to get sounded eerily like private recordings of Mingus singing his tunes at the piano.

He was a man in thrall to his passions, and supercharged feeling moved to the center of his music, for keeps. In Mingus's late-'50s bands of seven or more players, individual horns shouted back and forth like members of a rollicking church congregation on such numbers as "Wednesday Night Prayer Meeting." He'd motivate musicians by yelling encouragement and pushing them with his bass lines. Alas, he might also smack his horn players in the mouth when they fell short of expectations.

His love of counterpoint fit into his new concept. "Moanin'," from 1959, starts with Pepper Adams's baritone sax playing a bluesy theme, alone. On the repeats, more instruments and layers are added—two trombones plus drums; tenor sax and bass; alto sax and piano—until all nine players are in. Even after most of the horns fall away to make room for solos, Mingus keeps building the ensemble back up and breaking it down. Like his contemporary Max Roach (or Jelly Roll Morton before them), he prized varied dynamics and textures.

Mingus trained his drummer Dannie Richmond from scratch, and made especially good use of expressive saxophonists, including Texas tenor Booker Ervin and Roland Kirk. In the 1960s, Kirk became famous for playing two or three saxophones at the same time. (Wilbur Sweatman used to do it with clarinets.) Kirk also popularized the technique of circular breathing: inhaling through the nose while squeezing air out of the cheeks, to play continuously even while drawing a breath.

In 1960 Mingus formed a close bond with Eric Dolphy, a fellow Angeleno with an excitable sound on alto sax and bass clarinet who made a specialty of spectacular, lurching entrances. Dolphy had been influenced by Charlie Parker, but his aggressively angular lines earned him charter membership in the 1960s avant-garde. Mingus and Dolphy even improvised instrumental dialogues on stage, mimicking human speech. The bassist loved horns with the power of a human voice.

What did Miles Davis achieve in the 1950s? Who is Bill Evans?

Miles Davis's direction really came together in his hard bop 1955–'57 quintet, in which busy-sounding tenor saxophonist John Coltrane was his complementary opposite. On trumpet, Davis chose notes with great care, stayed mostly in the horn's middle range, and cultivated an introspective stance that sidestepped his technical limitations. No disgrace in that—why lead a band if not to play to your strengths?

In that period Davis had also started using the metal Harmon mute, which gave his playing a confidential quality, strikingly like the sound of his voice after he injured it around the same time. If any single sound signifies "jazz," it's Davis with a Harmon mute, and most trumpeters who use one either consciously or unconsciously pay tribute to him. An exception was cocky young phenomenon Lee Morgan, whose busy Harmon-muted solos radiate more overt cheer, as on "Bess" from 1960.

Unlike typical hard boppers, Davis retained an affection for pop songs, several borrowed from the trio repertoire of pianist Ahmad Jamal whose less-is-more aesthetic helped Davis articulate his own. Tired of bop's virtuoso steeplechases, he wanted to simplify.

In Paris in 1957, after disbanding his quintet, he improvised a soundtrack to Louis Malle's moody film noir *Elevator to the Scaffold*. Davis asked his accompanists to just play a couple of chords for him to improvise over, without a formal theme. He was inching toward a new style.

In 1958, Davis reunited his old quintet, plus alto saxophonist Cannonball Adderley. The following year, his quest for simplicity culminated in the most famous and most analyzed jazz album ever, *Kind of Blue*. The LP popularized "modal jazz," in which the players improvise off modes instead of goal-oriented chord sequences. Modes were the familiar major and minor scales, plus some less common ones inherited or derived from the ancient Greeks. Jazz improvisers had always fit appropriate scales to underlying chords, but a modal jazz tune might arbitrarily jump from one key center to another. On "So What" the players improvise on the D and E-flat minor scales. Those half-step shifts between keys are reminiscent of flamenco guitar music; the notes in the underlying minor 11th chords resemble the intervals between open guitar strings.

"Flamenco Sketches" was *Kind of Blue*'s most advanced piece, with no written melody, and five key centers. Specific modes were assigned, but the players weren't fastidious about sticking to them. The key centers were sequenced in a set order, but the players decided how long they held to them, usually 4 or 8 bars, before advancing to the next—which meant the rhythm players had to listen very carefully. On Coltrane's solo especially, pianist Bill Evans and bassist Paul Chambers seem to know where he's going before he gets there.

The challenge, Davis stressed, was to be melodically creative with minimal outside stimulation. This loosening of the harmonic straitjacket was part of a decisive postbop shift, to make structures more free and less confining.

His key ally on *Kind of Blue* was Bill Evans, who returned to the group to play on most of it, and who wrote the explanatory liner notes and some of the music. Evans had also been working with composer George Russell, who was preoccupied with the utility of the Lydian mode, with its built-in raised fourth—F♮ in the key of C, basically the flatted fifth (G♭) under another name.

Evans had exquisitely precise touch at the keys and deep knowledge of French impressionist harmony. These would soon be displayed in an enormously influential trio, with drummer Paul Motian and the tragically short-lived bass virtuoso Scott LaFaro; their quiet ballads would set a benchmark for subtlety in jazz.

A few months before *Kind of Blue*, Evans had begun a solo recording of Leonard Bernstein's ballad "Some Other Time" and became so transfixed by his two-chord introductory vamp that he stuck with it, spinning gossamer-wing improvised lines over it; five minutes in, he's doing high-note birdcalls. That standalone performance was dubbed "Peace Piece," and that same two-chord vamp would introduce "Flamenco Sketches." Improvisers are great recyclers of their own ideas. Evans's quiet intro to Chet Baker's "Alone Together" anticipates *Kind of Blue*'s moody "Blue in Green" recorded two months later.

The Spanish influence glimpsed on *Kind of Blue* was explicit on Davis's next big project, *Sketches of Spain*, one of four orchestral LPs arranged for him by *Birth of the Cool* ally Gil Evans (no relation to Bill). Record labels had started issuing LPs of global music, and some pieces were adapted from field recordings. "The Pan Piper" was based on a Peruvian Indian panpipe melody. "Saeta" is derived from a Spanish Holy Week procession, right down to the sound of a brass band approaching from and retreating into the distance (an echo of Charles Ives's Connecticut sketches). Softly bowed basses under Davis's expressive, open-ended solo recall Claude Thornhill's chords that hang in the air, an influence Gil Evans never tired of. He made beautiful records without Miles, too.

Davis's music had changed remarkably, from 1949 cool to 1955 hard bop to modal '59. No jazz musician was better at periodic reinvention—not even Coleman Hawkins, who'd gone from vaudeville corn in the 1920s to creamy swing-era balladry in the '30s and to a harder, all-business timbre in the late '50s. That last move was a response to such tough younger tenors as Coltrane and Sonny Rollins.

What's important about John Coltrane? Sonny Rollins?

In the late 1950s, the younger players nicknamed Trane and Newk were the major new voices on tenor saxophone. Both had apprenticed with Miles Davis and Thelonious Monk, and they'd sparred as friendly rivals on Rollins's "Tenor Madness" in 1956. And both, in the early '60s, would record with Ornette Coleman sidemen, looking for their own avenues into free jazz. Coltrane, born in 1926, was older by four years, but Rollins emerged sooner, debuting as a leader in '51, six years before Coltrane.

After Davis broke up his quintet in 1957, Coltrane played for seven months with Monk, whose style was as obstinately economical as Coltrane's was restlessly expansive. But the hectic phrases scattered in Monk's convoluted "Trinkle, Tinkle" were catnip to Coltrane; he loved odd rhythmic subdivisions because they allowed him to cram in more notes. Coltrane moved beyond triplets into quintuplets and then septuplets: seven notes squeezed into the space of a beat or two. Monk didn't mind Coltrane playing so many notes, as long as his improvisations developed out of or illuminated the source material.

"Trinkle, Tinkle" shows how even before *Kind of Blue* the saxophonist was obsessed with scales and chords, and he returned to Davis with new confidence. Davis used modes to simplify. Coltrane, by contrast, superimposed multiple scales over a single chord. On "Come Rain or Come Shine" under his own name, Coltrane stays close to Harold Arlen's lovely tune, but scalar runs shoot up between its phrases like bamboo. He both venerates the melody and succumbs to his obsessions. Coltrane had a fine sense of balance; his zillion-note runs are broken up and redeemed by regal, soaring long tones. In the frantic '60s he played touching ballads, in small groups with Duke Ellington or baritone crooner Johnny Hartman.

Coltrane digested (and popularized) musicologist Nicolas Slonimsky's thick book of hundreds of scales. His test pattern "Giant Steps," with short sequences of two or three chords that jumped from key to key, began as a practice exercise. But he soon set such obstacle courses aside, preferring modal jazz for flat-out sprinting.

There's a physicality to his scale-spinning. These sets of notes, ultimately derived from the acoustical overtone series, really got the horn's internal air column vibrating. That love of sheer saxophone sound is obvious on Coltrane's 1960 "Mr. Day," a blues anchored to an irresistible two-note figure, a rising minor third, the second note held long to let it ring, a heraldic gesture he returns to in his solo. A decade later, an ethnomusicologist visiting Burkina Faso would tape an unnamed West African musician on a homemade reed instrument fashioned from a millet stalk, a *bounkam*, playing two endlessly reiterated notes, as loopy and expressive as a Sonny Terry blues harmonica solo. It is curiously reminiscent of "Mr. Day." (See the discography section of this book for details.)

Coltrane was earnest, turning "My Favorite Things" from *The Sound of Music* into a modal thrash, without perceptible irony. Sonny Rollins, on the other hand, took evident delight in unlikely material: the 1922 flappers' fave "Toot-Toot-Tootsie," Broadway belter Ethel Merman's anthem "There's No Business like Show Business," and the faux-cowboy song "Wagon Wheels." But Rollins always had sound musical reasons for picking them—the syncopated stutter of "Tootsie," say. His 1957 take on Johnny Mercer's "I'm an Old Cowhand," with drummer Shelly Manne clip-clopping on woodblocks, has a jocular air alien to Coltrane.

"Wagon Wheels" and "Cowhand" are on Rollins's 1957 masterpiece *Way Out West* with its iconic William Claxton cover photo, depicting the saxophonist as a western gunslinger. The tune "Way Out West" ambles at a leisurely horseback lope and conveys the easy melodicism of a kids song, ending with a paraphrase of Bing Crosby's breezy "Swinging on a Star." But the 20-bar tune takes some weird turns, touching on several keys and all 12 notes in the chromatic scale. In his solo Rollins deconstructs its rhythms and melody in a way that's somehow good-natured and corrosive at once. That's very Monk-like, as is his appreciation for space. Rollins trills at length, barks out phrases, slurs and distorts his line, harps on a couple of braying figures, and shows off a gloriously bleating tone.

Way Out West was the first of several Rollins albums for tenor, bass, and drums trios, which gave him little room to hide and gave the bassist—Ray Brown in this case—a more pivotal role. Another stand-out is *Live at The Village Vanguard*, with Monk bassist Wilbur Ware and future Coltrane drummer Elvin Jones. Even now, tenors using the trio format will nod to Rollins in some way, just as jazz musicians playing calypsos refer to his 1956 "St. Thomas."

Between 1956 and '66, Rollins went through a few personal and stylistic changes. He took sabbaticals from the scene, led a quiet quartet including guitarist Jim Hall, flirted with free jazz, and staged a raucous face-off with Coleman Hawkins in which Sonny's crew tried to outfox the old master, who came back roaring. On record throughout this period, Rollins was at his peak, which is about as good as jazz gets.

How did jazz address the Civil Rights Movement of the 1950s and '60s?

Black entertainers were at the forefront of the movement, and racially integrated jazz bands spoke for themselves. *Black, Brown, and Beige* and similar Ellington compositions beamed with black pride; Billie Holi-day's 1939 "Strange Fruit" addressed the horrors of lynching.

But even in the '50s, musicians who spoke up for justice felt some resistance. In a note to his 1958 trio album *Freedom Suite*, Sonny Rollins wrote, "America is deeply rooted in Negro culture; its colloquialisms, its humor, its music. How ironic that the Negro, who more than any other people can claim America's culture as his own, is being perse-cuted and repressed."[2] Some white fans took exception to this mild observation.

By the 1950s, Louis Armstrong was thought to be too much the acquiescent and smiling black entertainer (his theme song was the sentimental "When It's Sleepy Time Down South"). But in 1957, he reacted to Arkansas governor Orval Faubus blocking the integration of

Little Rock schools by blasting him, President Eisenhower, and the secretary of state on whose behalf he'd been touring the world: "The way they are treating my people in the South, the government can go to hell."[3]

Two years later, bassist Charles Mingus brought his inflammatory "Fables of Faubus" to a session for the Columbia label, which balked at letting him sing the lyrics. He recorded the song, complete with lyrics, as "Original Faubus Fables" for Candid in 1960 in call-and-response with drummer Dannie Richmond:

> *Name me someone who's ridiculous, Dannie.*
> *—Governor Faubus!*
> *Why is he so sick and ridiculous?*
> *—He won't permit us in his schools.*
> *Then he's a fool!*
> *—Old fool!*

Mingus gave instrumental pieces provocative titles he might expound on, on stage: "Prayer for Passive Resistance," "Meditation on Integration," "Meditation (for a Pair of Wire Cutters)," "They Trespass the Land of the Sacred Sioux," and, later, "Remember Rockefeller at Attica."

John Coltrane patterned the cadences of 1963's prayerlike "Alabama" after Martin Luther King's memorial sermon for four girls killed in a Birmingham church bombing. He also played fundraisers for King.

No one fused the musical and political like drummer Max Roach, and nowhere more than on 1960's *We Insist! Freedom Now Suite,* with its cover photo of a lunch counter sit-in. A small pan-African percussion section including Nigeria's Michael "Babatunde" Olatunji and Bronx-born Ray Mantilla, of Puerto Rican extraction, layered interlocking patterns on "All Africa," as Abbey Lincoln sang out the names of tribal peoples. Oscar Brown Jr.'s lyrics for "Driva' Man" and "Freedom Day" pointedly evoked slavery and Emancipation. Lincoln sang "Driva' Man" like a field holler, as Coleman Hawkins played uncommonly raw tenor, and Roach slammed out a 5-beat rhythm, the last heavily accented beat like the lash of a whip.

Roach was mindful of the political implications of drumming—how it had been banned by slave owners who feared drums' communicative power, and how percussive Sunday rituals in Congo Square had kept West African culture alive in New Orleans. Roach took to playing solo pieces and, eventually, solo programs. In the '70s he formed the percussion group M'Boom! as a sort of updated drum choir.

It's no accident that activists Mingus and Roach were rhythm players who rethought their instruments' subservient roles. In the 1960s, the increasing liberation of bass and drums would be seen as having political implications. One kind of freedom mirrors another.

How did jazz contribute to the rise of "world music" around 1960? Has government policy influenced the development of jazz?

As the Cold War heated up in the 1950s, segregation poisoned the United States' reputation abroad. Propagandists saw how jazz could be an antidote. Willis Conover began broadcasting jazz programs on Voice of America, a godsend to fans in the Soviet bloc for decades. The State Department started sending racially integrated jazz bands, including Gillespie's, Armstrong's, Goodman's, and Ellington's, on world tours, accompanied by pointed talk about jazz as democracy in action. Some musicians abroad had already been thinking along those lines; World War II and its aftermath had brought American popular culture to Europe and Japan like never before.

These tours also had profound unintended consequences, when American musicians brought new sounds home with them. In 1961 guitarist Charlie Byrd toured South America, came back with Brazil's bossa nova, and turned saxophonist Stan Getz on to it. That melodic style with colorful chord changes was perfect for Getz, and the Brazilians' harmonic ideas were influenced by modern jazz, another feedback loop. Soon Getz's "Girl from Ipanema" was all over the radio. Before long even Coleman Hawkins made a token bossa nova record. In truth, the groundwork had been laid in Los Angeles a decade earlier by a sambas-and-saxophone quartet led by Brazilian guitarist Laurindo Almeida and altoist Bud Shank, conceived by bassist Harry Babasin.

In 1958, pianist Dave Brubeck toured the Middle East and India, stimulating his drummer Joe Morello's interest in meters with an odd number of beats per bar and in additive rhythm patterns, simple beats assembled into complex sequences. In Turkey Brubeck heard a tangy 2+2+2+3 9-beat folk rhythm and recast it into 1959's "Blue Rondo à la Turk," one of his quartet's many new odd-meter showcases. Their hit was altoist Paul Desmond's "Take Five" in 5/4 time, written to show off Morello.

The trick is to reduce complex meters to multiples of 2 and 3: to think of 5/4 as alternating bars of 2/4 and 3/4. But at first Brubeck played those 5/4s and 9/8s like he doggedly counted out every bar. He made odd-meter play sound like rocket science, describing it in the notes to his best-seller *Time Out* as "the result of weeks of concentration on a particular problem."[4] The quartet would get better at it later, expanded into 7- and 11-beat rhythms.

Max Roach's 1959 quintet had a blues that came out of jamming in 5/4, "As Long As You're Living," that sounded more natural and swinging. It was released as a single but didn't become a hit like "Take Five."

So Brubeck got credit for making sound hard what Roach got no credit for making sound easy.

In the '60s, Brubeck and Duke Ellington made records that registered their impressions of countries they visited, from a tourist point of view. Ellington and aide Billy Strayhorn also wrote pieces based on birdcalls heard in their travels, like Strayhorn's "Bluebird of Delhi (Mynah)." That feature for Jimmy Hamilton's tweeting clarinet appeared on Ellington's *Far East Suite,* tourist music of a very high order.

Some Americans had grown up with offshore sounds. Early jazz violinist Joe Venuti and guitarist Eddie Lang (born Salvatore Massaro) echoed the string traditions of their parents' native Italy. Calypso-loving Sonny Rollins's folks came from St. Thomas in the (U.S.) Virgin Islands. Horace Silver's penchant for Iberian-African rhythms was stimulated by his father, a violinist and guitarist born in Portugal's Cabo Verde islands off West Africa. The guitar-like two-note bass vamp that made Silver's 1964 "Song for My Father" a hit would propel Steely Dan's "Rikki Don't Lose That Number" a decade later. (See chap. 5 for more on jazz and world music.)

4
Jazz 1960–1980: The Avant-Garde and Its Aftermath

What is "avant-garde" jazz?

"Avant-garde" refers to a range of responses starting in the mid-1950s to familiar musical formulas, hard bop's in particular. "Free jazz" is often used as a synonym. In general, the avant-garde sought to loosen up forms: to get away from improvising over fixed chord sequences and from narrowly defined roles for bass and drums. It also embraced greater levels of dissonance.

That said, it's hard to generalize about the movement. John Coltrane's '60s bands played loud, frenetic "energy music," whereas clarinetist Jimmy Giuffre's trio improvised quietly. Though bop had been a collective effort to develop a coherent language, leaders like Coltrane, Ornette Coleman, Albert Ayler, and Cecil Taylor all had different approaches—which didn't prevent some of them from playing together on occasion.

Nowadays, the term "avant-garde" may also describe current styles reminiscent of that groundbreaking music, more than 50 years after it arrived.

Did free jazz break with jazz that came before it?

Some defenders and detractors alike say so, but no. It had been brewing for a while. In 1949, pianist Lennie Tristano's band with saxophonists Lee Konitz and Warne Marsh, who'd already been playing in spontaneous counterpoint over bebop chords, recorded two free improvisations. On the fast "Intuition" and slow "Digression," they kept the contrapuntal interplay but threw out the underlying song form. On both, Tristano starts solo, to set the tempo and mood, before saxes, guitar, and bass enter one at a time. The music can get dense as the players feel their way through, but the improvising never falls apart, and they manage coherent endings.

This spontaneous music worked because jazz musicians are usually close listeners, attentive to the harmonic implications of the notes their bandmates play, and they pull together to give the music a sense of direction. So too in free improvisation, though the musicians don't always want to make a songlike statement. They may superimpose distinctly different patterns on one another, or aim for a dense and static texture.

Other occasional free improvisations followed Tristano's. Drummer Shelly Manne's West Coast trio with trumpeter Shorty Rogers recorded "Abstract No. 1" in 1955, in which Jimmy Giuffre switches rapidly among tenor and baritone saxes and clarinet, anticipating 1960s Chicago "multi-instrumentalists." Those later Chicagoans would also perform unaccompanied solo horn concerts, but Coleman Hawkins had recorded "Picasso" for solo tenor sax in 1948, free-associating but drawing on long experience constructing memorable improvisations. Hawkins went on to record occasional solo pieces in the '50s, as did Giuffre and Sonny Rollins.

Free players didn't start from scratch. Ornette Coleman's alto saxophone sound was beholden to Charlie Parker. Bandleader Sun Ra's weird harmonies might resemble bop arranger Tadd Dameron's. (Dameron's dreamy, cosmic, erotic "Heaven's Doors Are Open Wide" from 1949 could almost be a Sun Ra tune.) Soprano saxophonist Steve Lacy and trombonist Roswell Rudd came to collectively improvised free jazz via dixieland, in which horns also interact in informal counterpoint, and they'd co-led an early-'60s band that played only Thelonious Monk tunes.

Some of the new breed's "extended techniques" harked back to freakish effects that early jazz inherited from vaudeville. Screaming high-energy saxophones were a staple of '40s rhythm and blues. Free jazzers were also fond of marches, reaching back to pre-jazz communal music.

Putting their own spin on old ideas led to new ones. Cecil Taylor's slambam piano style grew out of Ellington's and Monk's percussive attacks, Monk's and Dave Brubeck's thick and stubborn chords, Tristano's long intricate lines, and Horace Silver's terse left-hand punctuations. Coltrane's '60s music built on modal jazz he'd played with Miles Davis. *Kind of Blue*'s slow and beautiful "Flamenco Sketches," with no written melody and improvised sections of variable length, was already avant-garde.

Is free jazz like playing tennis without a net?

Free improvising—playing from scratch and discovering the music's form as it unfolds—is a special challenge. Players give up the security that comes from having fixed parameters to work from. It's more like trapeze work without a net.

Did Ornette Coleman's free jazz dispense with chord changes?

Sometimes, but not always. The music Coleman played with his piano-less, two-horn quartets beginning in 1959 was often based on conventional song forms, with melodies implying specific chord changes. But improvising on a theme, without a pianist sounding background chords, Coleman and his alter ego Don Cherry (who played "pocket trumpet," actually a compact cornet) were free to follow those chords and the scales they implied, or to deviate from them—though they had their pet licks like everyone else. They might suspend, stretch, or compress the form, linger on one chord, or play a line that suggests chords unrelated to the original tune. Coleman may play some bluesy lick and then repeat it in a different key, like Charlie Parker.

Ornette came from Fort Worth, in Texas, one state where blues evolved out of field hollers. His new approach had parallels to early blues musicians like singer Texas Alexander, who might jump to another key or skip a few bars in performance. Even contemporaries like Lightnin' Hopkins or John Lee Hooker might add or lose a bar or couple of beats, to accommodate a truncated or overstuffed lyric, or hold to one guitar chord when the vocal line implied a shift in harmony.

Coleman's and Cherry's unpredictable trajectories challenged their rhythm players the way Texas Alexander challenged guitarist Lonnie Johnson on record. Freed from the old role of marking out forms and chord changes, what might Coleman's crew do instead? Drummer Edward Blackwell became a master of punctuating Ornette's line endings with percussive commas, semicolons, and periods. Coleman's other drummer, Billy Higgins, absorbed many of Blackwell's ideas but was apt to just keep swinging, providing momentum one bar at a time. Bassist Charlie Haden might hover around a tune's key without committing to specific harmonies, or suggest the trajectory of simple chords moving away from and back toward home, as in the blues or Anglo-Scottish mountain songs.

As a child, Haden had sung with a family band in the so-called hillbilly tradition. On Coleman's 1959 "Ramblin'," he gets back to folk roots by strumming simple harmonies as if his upright bass were a guitar; his strummed solo breaks into the verse of the traditional ballad "Old Joe Clark." Behind him, Billy Higgins taps out high clipped cymbal sounds like a chuck-wagon triangle. Alto and cornet voice the melody—part Charlie Parker, part barn dance—in looser-than-bop unisons, yipping out phrase-capping high notes. On his solo, Ornette stretches notes like taffy, growling, bending pitches, holding them across several beats. When he pulls back, Haden switches from strumming to walking to maintain momentum. Coleman's singsong phrases can sound suavely bluesy or like the happy cry of a prospector finding a gold nugget. Cherry's solo picks up from Ornette's final phrase. His lines can be a little more polished, but there's a bugle in his raspy tone.

Before Coleman, no groundbreaking modernist had sounded so unabashedly rustic.

How did John Coltrane's music change in the '60s?

Coltrane's fascination with modes and scales led him to the music of India with its many complex ragas. He befriended sitar virtuoso Ravi Shankar years before the Beatles embraced him, even naming a son for him; Ravi Coltrane would grow up to play jazz saxophone. Besides tenor, John Coltrane started playing soprano sax, with a nasal tone like an Indian double-reed.

By 1960, he'd assembled the nucleus of the quartet he'd use for the next four years, pianist McCoy Tyner and drummer Elvin Jones. They were joined the following year by bassist Jimmy Garrison, who'd just quit Coleman's band. These comrades played with as much muscle and energy as he did. Coltrane was tireless. He'd play "My Favorite Things" for 45 minutes in a club and then practice backstage between sets. His single-minded devotion took on religious overtones, with song and album titles like "Dear Lord," "Song of Praise," *A Love Supreme*, and *Om*.

Tyner's big, wide-open chords created billowy backdrops for Coltrane without limiting his options. Elvin Jones was celebrated for his hyperactivity; he could play different rhythms with each limb, at high volume. But he also had a remarkably relaxed swing feel. Garrison might strum a bass part recalling the background drone of an Indian tambura, but with the intense physicality of a flamenco guitarist.

Coltrane was a great booster of other musicians, occasionally inviting fellow saxophonists, including Eric Dolphy and Pharoah Sanders, to share his bandstand. In time Coltrane inspired two diametrically opposed sets of disciples. He spawned high-energy players who scribbled on their horns; the speed and intensity of their improvised lines were more important than the actual pitches. Other followers diligently analyzed and systematized his harmonic choices, turning his style into a method. Those schools divided the heart and technical bravado that were inseparable in Coltrane's own music.

In the mid-'60s he was enamored of fellow tenor Albert Ayler's way of getting the vibrations moving, and Coltrane's later recordings show Ayler's influence: such tunes as "Ogunde" were simpler and more prayer-like, played rubato (without a fixed tempo) and with heavier vibrato. Ayler, along with Ornette Coleman, played at Coltrane's funeral in 1967.

What about Albert Ayler?

Playing saxophone duets in church with his father was a formative experience. Ayler loved a simple and impassioned melody, the wide and otherworldly vibrato gospel saxophonists get, and speaking-in-tongues rapture. In 1964 he recorded an album of spirituals.

A typical Ayler tune is a two- or three-chord ditty suggesting or quoting from bugle calls, folk dances, nursery rhymes, national anthems, or drinking songs—all community musics, as church music is. He was a populist who yearned to connect with the public. On his final studio sessions in 1969, he featured a soul singer and guitarist Henry Vestine from the blues-rock band Canned Heat. Ayler died under mysterious circumstances the following year.

The plasticity of his tenor saxophone sound was especially striking. Ayler's solos can be poignant, especially at slow tempos, but his improvised lines writhe like a snake. Overtone-drenched shrieks and emphatic amen low notes were cloaked in an exaggerated vibrato reminiscent of warbling clarinets soaring above New Orleans parade bands. It's a raw, profoundly human sound.

The trio he led in 1964 was one of the great jazz groups, at once extreme and basic. On its album *Spiritual Unity*, bass and drums are liberated from traditional timekeeping chores. "Ghosts (First Variation)" has an aphoristic, maddeningly catchy calypso melody taken at a fairly slow tempo. (Later versions are faster.) After that the collective improvising is wide open. The players don't try to follow the form or simple chords when they improvise, but Ayler often touches on or alludes to the melody to unify the performance.

In that free zone, there's no fixed tempo. The ways bassist Gary Peacock and drummer Sunny Murray embroider the time without stating an explicit beat obscures whether the underlying pulse is fast or slow. Peacock's pliable, sliding, string-thwacking approach matches Ayler's spontaneous distortions of the tune. Murray, who'd already worked with Cecil Taylor, plays long waves of sound on chattering cymbals, bending the beat the way his colleagues bend pitches. He doesn't have to play loud to be powerful. The trio's music had an intensity, fervor, and cohesion that's still hard to match.

Their style seemed to emerge fully formed. You can't hear it coming in Peacock's earlier, orderly work with cool groups or Bill Evans's or Paul Bley's piano trios. But Ayler's trio proved a tough act to follow. They added cornetist Don Cherry for a European tour, then disbanded. Albert's subsequent bands with brother Donald Ayler on trumpet and Michel Samson on violin had a lighter, dancing-'round-the-maypole joyfulness. The short tracks on the 1968 release *Love Cry* showcased Albert's catchy melodies. But the later stuff never touched that 1964 trio's extraordinary freedom.

How does Cecil Taylor's music work?

Taylor is among the most dissonant and kinetic of pianists. His hands can be a blur as he pummels the keyboard. His clusters are denser than Monk's. (His rambunctious 1955 take on Monk's "Bemsha Swing" was an early glimmer of the avant-garde.) Because of his unbridled athleticism and his rejection of 12- or 32-bar themes, some find Taylor's music anarchic, but it's highly organized.

In his pioneering musicological study of the new music, *Free Jazz*, Ekkehard Jost spends five pages dissecting Taylor's 17-minute septet performance "Unit Structure/As of Now/Section" from 1966.[1] Little kernels of melody are paraphrased, slowed, or transposed to another key, instantly or 10 minutes later. Short composed bits may break up or cue improvised statements lasting anywhere from a few seconds to several minutes. Soloists and rhythm players, including two bassists, one plucking and one bowing, sometimes move at different speeds.

It was a new and disorienting method, and yet his alter ego then and into the 1980s, whippet-fast alto saxophonist Jimmy Lyons, could sound uncannily like Charlie Parker.

Behind all the speed and complexity, Taylor's music is rooted in the basics: themes and variations, and call-and-response. On later solo recitals, such as 1986's *For Olim*, he may start a sequence with a little nugget of a theme, expand on it and transform it, then distill it into a new kernel and start again. The act of performance becomes an organic process.

In the 1990s, Taylor rehearsed his musicians by teaching them short thematic figures he'd use as building blocks on the gig. He trained players to recognize and respond to such kernels on the bandstand, where he (and they) might play or paraphrase them in any order, key, or tempo.

What did Sun Ra contribute?

The space-age bandleader and keyboardist was always ahead of his time. Even in the mid-'50s, he and a half dozen or so acolytes would collectively improvise music tethered to minimal predetermined material, like the bass ostinato (repeating figure) and kettle drum beat on 1956's "Call for All Demons." That same year he recorded the modal "India" for percussion and electric piano. In that period he also used electric bass, an instrument rare in jazz at the time. Ra also spontaneously conducted his band in performance, using hand gestures to cue soloists and sections in and out, and drawing the shape of a spontaneous melody in the air.

Yet his roots went back to the dawn of the swing era. As a teenager he transcribed a Fletcher Henderson chart, before Benny Goodman hired Fletcher, and in the late '40s Ra worked as Henderson's deputy arranger and pianist for a few months in Chicago. Like Duke Ellington, Sun Ra would complicate saxophone overtones by giving low saxes high notes and high saxes low notes.

Ra's compositions are often pleasantly hypnotic. In the '50s his rhythms might evoke faux-Polynesian "bachelor pad" records, exotica from some nebulous nowhere. That fit. By his testimony, he had visited Saturn and come to realize he was not really of this planet. Sun Ra's earth music was like a second language; he sometimes improvised solutions outside the norms.

For clarity and transparency, conventional horn arrangers space notes widely at the bottom of a chord and bunch them closer together at the top. Ra would do the opposite, for more opaque textures. "Moon Dance" (1963) for electric organ, bass, and drums finds a groove far removed from Jimmy Smith's organ trios. It's weird and singular, less for Ra's ghostly melodies and brooding or screechy chords than for relentless two-chord bass vamping and drummer Clifford Jarvis's too-loud and emphatic syncopations at the center of the music like a melody.

Sun Ra could play the wise fool in concert, with his Arkestra's gaudy costumes and pageantry, conga lines through the audience and pro-galactic sing-alongs like "Space Is the Place" and "Interplanetary Music." But no avant-gardist was as comfortable marshaling large forces.

It was a rite of passage for movement leaders to record with a big free band. Ornette Coleman had a double quartet—two of every-thing—on the 1960 album *Free Jazz*, playing short themes, organically developed, in spontaneous call-and-response. John Coltrane's 1965 *Ascension* was ecstatic roof-raising for 11 players. Cecil Taylor was guest soloist with the Jazz Composers Orchestra in 1968.

Sun Ra's big piece was 1965's loose and episodic *The Magic City* for around a dozen players: a heady mix of the ancient, futuristic, and con-temporary. Wood flutes and log drums evoke old-world Africa, state-of-the-art electronic keyboards and exaggerated reverb provide sci-fi effects, and once in a while horns break into squealing cacophony on cue. His Arkestra was close-knit and rehearsed daily; he jealously guarded saxophonists other leaders hired on the rare occasions when they could, tenor John Gilmore and alto Marshall Allen.

Ra's '60s music could also get very spare. "Cluster of Galaxies" paints the emptiness of the cosmos: gongs, wood drums, and a lyre clatter against a drop cloth of tape-deck reverb. He usually documented his music himself, selling LPs on his El Saturn label at gigs. The way they're recorded, from remote perspectives, with cavernous echo, contributes to the unearthly effect. He paints moods as effectively as any jazz composer after Ellington.

On gigs from the mid-1970s on, he'd break up the chants, space music, and synthesizer blast-offs with invigorating and surprisingly faithful versions of pieces from Henderson's or Ellington's book, orbiting back to his roots.

What is mainstream jazz? How did the mainstream react to the avant-garde?

By the 1960s the term "mainstream," coined in the '50s by critic Stanley Dance, had come to mean the swing-to-bop continuum of players who swung over chord changes, making music more modern than dixieland, but less radical than the avant-garde. For all their differences, swing and bop stars had long since demonstrated they could solo on the same tunes with the same rhythm section, without problems, as on the staged jam sessions of the very popular Jazz at the Philharmonic all-star tours of the late '40s and the '50s.

Also, by the 1960s bebop and hard bop were increasingly conflated into one big encompassing bop. (Cool was largely passé.) Bop had become solidly mainstream, and some boppers dismissed free players for sidestepping the swing-and-changes jazz proficiency test. But other boppers leaned toward the new music.

At the prestigious Blue Note record label, which had been solidly hard bop in the '50s, altoist Jackie McLean's music became a sometimes hectic mix of old and new, with boppish melodies followed by loosely modal blowing. (Any improvising over slow or static chord changes came to be classified as modal.) On McLean's 1959 "Quadrangle," a pianoless, nominally open section was inspired by Ornette Coleman, but bassist Paul Chambers defaulted to "I Got Rhythm" chords anyway. In the early '60s, McLean got more rhythmically free, replacing piano with Bobby Hutcherson's ringing and dissonant vibes and adding the explosive, polyrhythmic teenage drummer Tony Williams.

Blue Note pianist Andrew Hill similarly freed up his bop, composing ear-worm tunes with elongated or compressed forms, 14 or 30 bars instead of the usual 12 or 32. Or he'd move the downbeats around by shifting between even and odd time signatures. On his 1964 "Flight 19," bop trumpeter Kenny Dorham, free-leaning bass clarinetist Eric Dolphy and in-between tenor saxophonist Joe Henderson leapfrog short improvised statements. Behind them, piano, bass, and drums double and halve the tempo so often you forget if it's a fast tune with slow parts or a slow one with fast parts. The drummer here too was Tony Williams; he would bring that same ambiguous alternation of fast and slow pulses to Miles Davis's "R.J." 10 months later.

How did Miles Davis react to the avant-garde?

It was complicated. Davis belittled its stars, but by 1965 he'd assembled a band of younger players sympathetic to its aims: drummer Tony Williams, bassist Ron Carter, pianist Herbie Hancock, and tenor saxophonist Wayne Shorter, who dug Coltrane's scalar approach, but rigorously edited his own ideas for a more elliptical sound.

As on *Birth of the Cool* or *Kind of Blue*, Davis collaborated with his musicians to find a new approach. The quintet built on *Kind of Blue*'s flexible forms and harmony, but with many new variations, like assigning different soloists different modes to improvise from. They'd spontaneously distort the forms and reduce composed melodies to free-floating scraps of material. On Shorter's "Nefertiti," he and Davis just play the one-line melody over and over, no solos, as drums boil over behind them.

Shorter's pieces pointed the way, and soon they were all composing like him, with Davis editing their pieces to highlight their best ideas. Davis tore apart and reassembled his 1961 "Drad Dog," itself a sort of remake of *Kind of Blue*'s "Blue in Green," to make a more focused piece with the same quiet 6/8 feel, "Circle."

Tony Williams drove the band from behind with crashing accents and monstrously efficient rapid timekeeping on cymbals. He exercised uncommon discretion over tempos and the general energy level. Only 17 when he joined Davis's band, he was young enough to embrace rockish 8th-note phrasing, even as his rapid swishing cymbals maintained a springy jazz feel.

For the 1966 album *Miles Smiles*, the quintet recorded much the way Bob Dylan did in the same period. After running down the melody a few times, they'd roll tape, and if Davis didn't cut them off before his solo was over, it was a take, flaws and all—an aggressive way to keep things spontaneous. The melody of Shorter's "Dolores" is one phrase repeated intermittently over fast bass and drums. Wayne starts out playing it alone, then the trumpeter joins him in careless unison, ragged but right. Hancock is unheard except for his hornlike solo, played entirely with one hand, a long, snaky line recalling Lennie Tristano. The band hadn't worked out an ending in advance, so Davis and Shorter improvise one, playing a game of tag with the opening phrase.

Mark Gridley's standard college text, *Jazz Styles: History and Analysis*, charts the convolutions in 1967's "Masqualero."[2] During the improvising, the basic ABA form morphs into AB, ABAA, or AABAA at times. Shorter's solo runs 10 extra bars, and there's a celebrated moment around 3:40 when Carter switches to waltz time, and bass, piano, and drums are in three different time signatures (3/4, 4/4, and 8/8), layering rhythms like West African drummers.

Davis's men kept pushing him further out, while Shorter's and Hancock's own Blue Note albums were tamer. Finally Davis reined them in. He introduced funkier rhythms, made Hancock and Carter play electric piano and bass sometimes, and tapped guest guitarists including George Benson. Davis was going electric.

What's the relationship between jazz and rock music in the 1960s?

Post-Beatles rock took a huge bite out of jazz record sales, which made for some rock-hostile jazz musicians. But rockers at least paid lip service to jazz. The Byrds' drummer Mike Clark, no virtuoso, professed admiration for Joe Morello and Elvin Jones. The perpetrators of the too-fast guitar solo on the Byrds' "Eight Miles High" and the vamp-based guitar and organ noodling on the Doors' "Light My Fire" declared those episodes to be Coltrane-inspired. Frank Zappa had his noisy improvised freak-outs. English rockers, raised on American blues, came off as better improvisers. The Zombies' "Time of the Season" had spare, impeccably timed B-3 organ solos by Rod Argent. Power trio Cream's long jam on bluesman Skip James's "I'm So Glad" stepped up to the brink of free improvisation, almost dissolving the song's form. Cream bassist Jack Bruce made *Things We Like,* a rare convincing jazz album by a rock star.

Jazz musicians employed in recording studios got pop work. Bud Shank played flute on the Mamas and the Papas' hit "California Dreamin'." Drummer Herbie Lovell played smashing tom-tom fills behind Gordon Lightfoot and Peter, Paul, and Mary, and was among the jazz musicians on Bob Dylan's first single with a band, 1962's "Mixed-Up Confusion."

Meanwhile, Count Basie, Duke Ellington, Ella Fitzgerald, and others recorded Beatles songs. Pianist Ramsey Lewis covered mid-'60s rock hits like "The 'In' Crowd" in live trio versions, with the audience sing-ing along. From 1968 Woody Herman's big band, still on the road, played "Proud Mary" and covers of songs by the Doors, Burt Bacharach, Stevie Wonder, and James Taylor. Singer and pianist Nina Simone lifted Dylan, Leonard Cohen, and Judy Collins tunes off Collins's albums.

Drawing on rock rhythms, jazz drummers hit a heavy backbeat and developed the boogaloo rhythm popularized by Lee Morgan's much-imitated "The Sidewinder," a jukebox hit recorded in 1963. Billy Higgins played the signature snare-drum pattern that mediated between rock and Cuban music: rockish 8th notes with heavy accents on the third and sixth beats for syncopated snap, accompanied by jazzy sizzle on ride cymbal.

Many jazz guitarists held to bop's pick-heavy attack and muted tone in an age of Jimi Hendrix's writhing sustain. But Sun Ra investigated new electronic keyboards, finding what each was good for. (Organ groups were electric bands too.) Eddie Harris found what worked on the Varitone, a tenor sax with some guitar-type sound modifiers attached, such as its ability to double his line an octave lower. He used that shadowing brilliantly, playing twisty variations on blues cries and gospel moans on "Listen Here" over a very danceable Latin-inflected medium groove.

How did jazz and rock combine in the 1970s?

Miles Davis flirted with electric instruments in the last phase of his Shorter-Hancock-Carter-Williams quintet, whose members started defecting in 1968. After the spacious jams on *In a Silent Way* in '68 and *Bitches Brew* in '69, Davis dived all the way into busy electric music in 1970, playing hippie palaces Fillmore East and West. The crunchy dis-tortion of sideman Chick Corea's electric piano sounded like Cecil Taylor in overdrive. To be heard above loud keyboards, Wayne Shorter began playing soprano sax with a focused, nasal tone akin to Coltrane's.

Davis's early '70s funk gave other jazz musicians cover to plug in, but it disgusted many longtime fans. His electric bands had less to do with bop than with James Brown's jittery 16th-note funk and Sly and the Family Stone's funk pop. Davis's sometime guitarist John McLaughlin put the sound of wah-wah pedal in his ear, and the trumpeter began using one in 1970. The device had been invented to let guitarists imitate plunger-muted horns, but Davis wasn't trying to do Bubber Miley; he'd work the pedal slowly for an oozing sound instead.

Davis made good salads from odd ingredients. "Black Satin" from 1972 begins and ends with short sequences for sitar and tabla, sounds of India. Between those bookends is electric funk: wah-wah Davis toys with a chipper, whistling workman's hook over distorted keyboards, sleigh bells, and flamenco-style handclaps.

This new jazz-rock was dubbed "fusion." One of its engines was Yorkshire-born guitarist McLaughlin, who did for India's additive rhythms what Brubeck had done for Turkish beats a decade before. McLaughlin's electric quintet Mahavishnu Orchestra popularized loud, fast, rhythmically complex fusion; unlike many bands that followed, Mahavishnu made it sound more like music than finger exercise. Bandleader Don Ellis was even more enamored of Indian-style additive rhythms. His 1968 blues "Beat Me Daddy, Seven to the Bar," had a 43-beat, 7+7+7+7+8+7 rhythm pattern the length of an entire chorus.

Davis's old gang went fusion. Shorter cofounded and gradually vanished into the band Weather Report, eclipsed by synthesizer wiz Joe Zawinul and, for a time, the very influential Jaco Pastorius on slippery-sounding fretless bass guitar. Chick Corea formed the band Return to Forever. Herbie Hancock was reborn as a dance music specialist on funky jams like "Chameleon," built on a fat catchy bass vamp.

Their old fans might have cheered their financial success, but generally they didn't. For some folks, jazz is like the Mafia: once you're in, stepping out is betrayal. Still, in the mid-'70s, even Ornette Coleman went electric, forming a septet with two guitarists, two electric bassists, and two drummers. That group, Prime Time, provided him a spiky new setting for his tunes, although his alto sound and approach to improvising remained the same. But all these musicians who embraced electric jazz would either continue to play acoustic jazz or would return to it, if only briefly.

Did jazz almost die out in the 1970s? Who is Keith Jarrett? Paul Bley? Carla Bley?

Major record labels lost interest as sales declined, and the hard bop mainstream went into eclipse. Art Blakey's Jazz Messengers were notably less busy, a fact frequently cited by '70s doomsayers. It's more accurate to say that the jazz styles that did flourish, such as fusion or the glossy, lightly funky sound promulgated by CTI Records, were not to their liking.

Although Ornette Coleman's vintage music with its shifting harmonic foundation was piano-resistant, his influence was plain on the music of another of Davis's former keyboard players, the very popular Keith Jarrett. His early '70s "American quartet" had drummer Paul Motian, who'd played in Bill Evans's classic trio, and two Coleman veterans, bassist Charlie Haden and tenor saxophonist Dewey Redman. Jarrett's folksy themes might recall Coleman's; his rolling piano style had roots in Paul Bley, the first pianist to successfully find a role in Coleman's music, on a 1958 nightclub engagement. Bley's mix of open harmony and linear improvising was to Coleman what Bud Powell was to Charlie Parker.

Like Bley, Jarrett started recording for Germany's ECM label, which began documenting his improvised solo concerts. These were often inventive and tuneful, if sometimes marred by precious self-indulgence. He also had an unfortunate tendency to sing along with himself in the voice of Jerry Lewis's nutty professor. For Continental tours, Jarrett formed a second band, his "European quartet" of Scandinavian ECM regulars. Norwegian tenor saxophonist Jan Garbarek's icy sound contrasted with Dewey Redman's bluesy warmth, but otherwise the two quartets were not so very different.

In the '70s ECM became a successful brand and developed a mannered house style. The music was drenched in studio reverb, and albums often started slowly and quietly, gradually building in intensity, volume, and speed, like the millennia-old classical music of India. What was really, really old was new again.

Also in the '70s, Carla Bley emerged as a leader of playful bands. In the early '60s, then-husband Paul Bley had encouraged her to compose, and she soon emerged as a fresh writer for Jimmy Giuffre's trio with Paul and for Paul's small groups. Carla had a gift for poplike melodic hooks she'd subject to her own catchy variations, grist for improvisers. A case in point is her "Ida Lupino," which begins with two short, shapely phrases in call-and-response formation—a tune inspired, she said, by doo-wop group Frankie Valli and the Four Seasons.

Soon Carla Bley was also composing and arranging for large ensembles. She wrote an album-length suite for vibraphonist Gary Burton, 1967's *A Genuine Tong Funeral*. For Charlie Haden's occasional Liberation Music Orchestra, her arrangements of revolutionary marches and anthems echoed politically progressive German composer Kurt Weill. By 1977 she was leading her own smaller big band of about ten pieces, playing her ballads, marches, anthems, and comic novelties.

What is the AACM? Who is Muhal Richard Abrams? Anthony Braxton? What is the Art Ensemble of Chicago?

Several potent strains of 1970s jazz had roots in Chicago in 1965 when the Association for the Advancement of Creative Musicians was founded. The AACM, an African American self-help co-op, rethought the avant-garde program.

New York free jazz tended to be dense, loud, and frenetic, no matter how much Albert Ayler's, Cecil Taylor's, and John Coltrane's music differed in particulars. The Chicago style of Roscoe Mitchell's 1966 recording *Sound* and Anthony Braxton's 1968 album *3 Compositions of New Jazz* was quiet and spacious. Silence carried as much weight as sound. Braxton's co-op trio with violinist Leroy Jenkins and trumpeter Leo Smith didn't even have a rhythm section. Members of the AACM were often "multi-instrumentalists," and Braxton and Mitchell played clarinets and saxes of various sizes. Horn players were encouraged to perform solo recitals. Chicagoans also used "little instruments"— toys, noisemakers, large gongs, a rack of hubcaps—to expand the sound spectrum.

Guided by pianist, composer, and former hard bopper Muhal Richard Abrams, the AACM's working-class members composed original music that moved freely among jazz, classical, marches, spirituals, electronica, and any other genre they studied or fancied. They were postmodern before the term was a buzzword.

They were also idealists who ran a school for young musicians and responded to Coltrane's spirituality. The Art Ensemble of Chicago, the AACM's flagship group, began every concert silently facing east, with some members face-painted and robed to evoke West Africa. But five minutes later they might be indulging trumpeter Lester Bowie's penchant for barbershop humor or playing a super-loose version of a Charlie Parker tune or one of Mitchell's widely zigzagging lines.

Like Mitchell, Braxton favored a blunt, staccato saxophone sound and written or improvised lines whose unpredictable leaps defeated a sense of tonality. Braxton thought less in terms of underlying chords than intersecting lines in four-way counterpoint. He was a prolific composer who recorded often in the '70s (and ever after): solo alto, wind trios, two-horn quartets with bass and drums, big bands, four symphony orchestras playing at once. His "Opus 58" for big band is a Sousa march that takes a wrong turn up a blind alley and bumps into a wall.

The AACM inspired St. Louis's short-lived Black Artists Group and caused a major rethink of what acceptable instrumentation might be. From now on, bands that tweaked or discarded traditional line-ups would become common.

Braxton tapped three members of the Black Artists Group to play a 1974 piece for four saxophones. Those three—Julius Hemphill, Oliver Lake, and Hamiet Bluiett—went on to form the World Saxophone Quartet with David Murray, and Hemphill became its principal composer. California's AACM-inspired ROVA saxophone quartet sprung up at the same moment. After them, into the '80s, came other sax quartets, similar wind choirs including the quartet Clarinet Summit, and Lester Bowie's Brass Fantasy, a sort of hip drum and bugle corps playing original music and old and new radio pop.

Julius Hemphill, an altoist from Fort Worth like Coleman, also played in small combinations with Abdul Wadud, who plucked or sawed his cello with the earthiness of a blues guitarist. Oliver Lake recorded on alto with three astringent violins, and with his reggae-inspired dance band Jump Up. The AACM (and ex-Basie) trombonist George Lewis became interested in interactive electronics: computers you could program to improvise with you.

For all the AACM's emphasis on original material, the Chicagoans honored the past. A Braxton-Abrams duo and Henry Threadgill's pianoless trio Air recorded Scott Joplin rags and helped set the stage for 1980s neoclassicism.

How did bop make a comeback? How did Dexter Gordon and Betty Carter contribute?

In the midst of the avant-garde's '70s second wave, there were intimations of a bop revival. Tenor saxophonist Dexter Gordon, who'd moved to Europe in the pre-Beatles early '60s, had frequently returned to the States to tour and record. But his 1976 album recorded live at New York's Village Vanguard, *Homecoming*, was given a major push by Columbia Records and was greeted as if Gordon had just returned from Mars. In his wake, friend and fellow expatriate tenor Johnny Griffin also enjoyed renewed attention in the States. West Coast bop altoist Art Pepper, off the scene for most of two decades owing to narcotics problems, made a spectacular comeback, his bebop burning with free-jazz intensity.

One great bopper who'd suffered lean times but had never gone away was singer Betty Carter. She was typical of older musicians who deplored the avant-garde for losing touch with jazz's core African American audience. Yet she drew on the new music's free approach to forms.

Carter didn't have a gorgeous voice like Ella Fitzgerald or Sarah Vaughan. It could be a little thin and reedy, and she didn't always clearly articulate lyrics. But her timing was exquisite. Like the early beboppers who inspired her, Carter liked her fast tunes very fast and her slow ballads very slow. A single song could move in many directions. On a 25-minute "Sounds (Movin' On)," cut live with her trio in 1979, she sings the melody very fast, very slowly, in a 4/4 medium groove and swinging 5/4; she gets loud, she gets very quiet, and she does some very rapid scatting.

On stage, her musicians watched her carefully for subtle signals and behind-the-back hand cues to divine where she'd jump next. From moment to moment they might tighten up on the beat or get loose and splashy. In the '90s she was belatedly hailed as a cultivator of young talent to rival Art Blakey, but in truth her apprenticeship program was more demanding.

What is "European improvised music"? Did American musicians participate?

European jazz musicians had steadily improved by the 1950s and '60s, and touring American soloists could find reasonably reliable backing in Paris, Amsterdam, Copenhagen, Stockholm, and elsewhere. Those rhythm sections might include American expatriates such as drummer Kenny Clarke and pianist Kenny Drew. American saxophonists living in Europe, among them Sidney Bechet, Don Byas, and Dexter Gordon, helped local players refine their concepts.

A few Americans who spent time on the Continent drew on European music too. In 1951 Stan Getz recorded a Swedish folk tune as "Dear Old Stockholm," inspiring saxophonist Lars Gullin to inject a folky Swedish flavor into his own music, two decades before the ECM label began cultivating a Scandinavian jazz sound.

The outbreak of free jazz in the 1960s particularly inspired some younger Western Europeans. If Albert Ayler (who'd been stationed in Germany as a GI) could write tunes incorporating "O Tannenbaum" and "La Marseillaise," why shouldn't they confront their own musical heritage? And if some free jazzers ignored the tune during the improvising, why start with a tune at all?

In the later '60s, likeminded Europeans sought each other out to improvise from scratch, among them English guitarist Derek Bailey and saxophonist Evan Parker, German saxophonist Peter Brötzmann and bassist Peter Kowald, Dutch pianist Misha Mengelberg and drummer Han Bennink, and the Danish Congolese saxophonist John Tchicai, who had played on Coltrane's *Ascension*.

More colleagues joined in, and the players began to notice how each country seemed to breed a distinct approach. English improvisers were quiet and cooperative, playing short, flinty gestures that formed an abstract mosaic. Germans loved a dense, high-energy onslaught, evident on Brötzmann's evocatively titled album *Machine Gun.* The Dutch were playfully antagonistic; they liked the friction between incompatible players. Bennink was a fast, loud swinger and noisemaker. Mengelberg loved Thelonious Monk's unhurried plunk, and the against-the-grain but internally logical chord sequences of forgotten '50s pianist Herbie Nichols.

Although the Dutch didn't observe the rule for long, swinging was forbidden: this was European improvised music, not jazz. There was very little blues in it. The Vietnam War had made sounding American uncool. And yet, trumpet and saxophone might play a little tune, followed by solos over piano, bass, and drums, before playing the tune again at the end. Jazz wasn't so easy to shake off.

Derek Bailey insisted his improvising was non-idiomatic, style-less, but no one had a more recognizable, atomistic style than he did. He sounded like he was methodically reducing his guitar to splinters. The Dutch, English, and German schools have continued to thrive and proliferate since. In time younger Scandinavian players came along, choosing from a smorgasbord (their term) of approaches.

One prime cultivator of European talent starting in the mid-'60s was cornetist Don Cherry, who had lived on the Continent off and on since leaving Ornette Coleman. Cherry's seductive, bugling post-Ayler tunes were a call to assemble for international musicians. His bands included Parisians, German vibraphonist Karl Berger, rapturous Argentine tenor saxophonist Gato Barbieri—Ayler reborn as a feverish romantic—and drummers from Turkey and Sweden.

Cherry also played with bassist Johnny Dyani, one of a group of exiles from apartheid South Africa scattered across northwestern

Europe, including trumpeter Mongezi Feza and altoist Dudu Pukwana, who had some of Coleman and Cherry's beautifully ragged rapport, and Abdullah Ibrahim, whose rolling piano polyrhythms evoked drum choirs and gospel music. In England, Holland, and Denmark, South Africans popularized jazz tunes with the flavor of *kwela*, the tuneful, easy-chord pennywhistle music of the black townships: a fresh injection of African content without American mediation.

In 1966, Steve Lacy, another American in exile, had a free improvising quartet with Dyani, South African drummer Louis Moholo, and Italian trumpeter Enrico Rava, who had his own romantic take on Cherry and Miles Davis. Based in Paris from 1970, Lacy formed durable partnerships with among others the Swiss-French violinist and vocalist Irene Aebi.

In the early '70s Lacy began playing solo concerts, often featuring Thelonious Monk tunes, an inspiration for his own unhurried singsong compositions and close-interval ensemble harmonies. He'd also play tunes by Monk and Herbie Nichols with Holland's Mengelberg and Bennink in the 1980s.

5
Jazz after 1980: The Postmodern Period

What's so important about Wynton Marsalis?

The New Orleans–born trumpeter's bravura technique made him an instant sensation while he was still in his teens, and, like teenage prodigy Lee Morgan in the 1950s, he chose Art Blakey's Jazz Messengers over Juilliard. From the first, Marsalis was notoriously outspoken in interviews, and his harsh condemnations of electric and free jazz polarized fans and critics. Since the 1990s he has directed jazz programming at the Lincoln Center in New York, which added to the controversy over his opinions. (More about that in connection with the '90s "jazz wars.")

The impressive debut *Wynton Marsalis*, recorded in 1981, bespoke his admiration for Miles Davis's 1960s quintet. He even performed the quintet's "R.J." with that band's rhythm section. Unlike earlier players, who asserted their individuality, Marsalis and his tenor saxophonist, brother, and fellow Messenger, Branford Marsalis, paid frank homage to Davis and Wayne Shorter.

For young Wynton, going back to vintage Davis was the way forward. Like a 1940s dixieland revivalist, he denounced the jazz of the previous 20 years as a betrayal of old ideals. He excoriated Davis's recent funk, denounced avant-gardists as charlatans, and championed the notion that swing and blues feeling were far more important than innovation. Similar to the president at the time, Ronald Reagan, he decried '60s permissiveness and advocated traditional values.

Marsalis's prime mentor was African American intellectual Albert Murray, whose 1976 book *Stomping the Blues* spelled out his views. Jazz tradition is a constant dialogue between the present and the past: "It is . . . far more a matter of imitation and variation and counter-statement than of originality."[1] For Murray, jazz train songs are about other train songs more than actual trains.

Still, some of Murray's Kansas City heroes held originality in higher esteem than he did. "Originality is the thing," Lester Young said. "You can have tone and technique and a lot of other things but without originality you ain't really nowhere."[2] Or as Basie trumpeter Buck Clayton put it, "If you don't do something new, then you might as well forget it."[3]

In 1986 Wynton Marsalis moved out of Davis's shadow with a new quartet, with Marcus Roberts on piano and the explosive Jeff "Tain" Watts, a holdover, still on drums. *Live at Blues Alley* displayed a brand of showmanship that is all about masterful technique and avoids empty gestures. Later albums, including 1991's *Uptown Ruler* for a new quintet with Roberts, were similarly dynamic. By then Marsalis had also been delving into New Orleans jazz, and had begun writing for a big band.

On that score his new idol was Duke Ellington, though his homages had an air of pastiche—like the comedic Rutles rearranging pilfered bits of Beatles songs. Marsalis's theme to the 1990 film

Tune in Tomorrow, "Big Trouble in the Easy," combined the swaggering gait of Duke's *Anatomy of a Murder* theme with birdlike clarinet à la Strayhorn's "Bluebird of Delhi." Albert Murray's views on train songs aside, Marsalis's 1998 "The Caboose" for big band is memorable not for evoking locomotive Ellingtonia but catching the sound of a train itself; a very specific slow-freight *da-dum-ka-dum* beat runs underneath.

Marsalis's writing continues to reference jazz's rich past. On 2003's *The Magic Hour* for nimble quartet, "You and Me" suggests the influence of hyperarranged little swing bands of the 1930s like John Kirby's. There are interlocking handclap patterns, a kidworthy 2-beat tune, bowed bass throughout, and two trumpet solos in contrasting voices (muted and open horn). Marsalis's compositions are most notable for their postmodern juxtapositions and rhythmic dexterity. His melodies don't linger in your ear, as two songs for singers on the same album make plain.

As a player, the mature Wynton is a master of trumpet voices. He can whisper like Davis and shout like Armstrong. He can play soft veiled tones, low blues moans deflected by a derby mute, ghostly falsettos, chicken cackles, and throaty squeals squarely on pitch. He's a show-off, but why hide all that?

Who were "the young lions"?

The title of the 1958 film (from Irwin Shaw's novel) entered the jazz lexicon as the name of a 1960 album featuring Lee Morgan and Wayne Shorter. In the '80s the term was revived to describe a flood of players who came along in Wynton's wake. Some—like trumpeter Terence Blanchard and saxophonist Donald Harrison, schooled in New Orleans alongside the Marsalises—retraced the brothers' own trajectory: a brief period of apprenticeship with Art Blakey (for others it was Betty

Carter) followed by a major-label recording contract. These serious young players wearing natty suits were also known as neoclassicists, neoconservatives, or neotraditionalists. Their emergence marked a significant generational shift. Previously, bop musicians had apprenticed for years before venturing out on their own. The trumpeter who Wynton Marsalis had replaced with Art Blakey, Valery Ponomarev, was 18 years older.

When Marsalis denounced the free and funky, some observers assumed he spoke for the many young lions who benefited from his success. But a number of those he worked with or mentored, including brother Branford, bassist Christian McBride, and trumpeters Blanchard, Roy Hargrove, and Nicolas Payton, went on to pursue funk/electric projects. Musicians who grew up on rock, funk, and hip-hop were generally less judgmental about pop than those jazz musicians whose livelihoods suffered when '60s rock came in.

How are modern jazz musicians educated?

From the 1920s on, jazz musicians mostly got their education on the road, from more experienced players or outstanding peers. Beboppers Charlie Parker and Dizzy Gillespie apprenticed in big swing bands like Jay McShann's and Cab Calloway's, and began to shape their new music at informal jam sessions. In either setting, ideas were exchanged and peer-reviewed; weaknesses were exposed and eliminated or compensated for. There were also a few high school teachers grooming future professionals, notably Chicago's Walter Dyett and Los Angeles's Lloyd Reese.

With the waning of the big bands after World War II, jam sessions became even more important as information exchanges. In various cities there are still sessions at which elders school young hopefuls, like saxophonist Von Freeman's legendary Tuesday nights in Chicago bars.

A shift from this informal education to college-level jazz pedagogy got rolling in the 1970s at institutions like Boston's New England Conservatory and Berklee College of Music. But jazz education's influence really became apparent in the '80s as college programs proliferated in the United States and abroad with the rise of well-trained young lions. The masters' great solos were transcribed for study, and myriad ways to get from one dense chord to the next were mapped out. As a consequence, some lions were longer on technique than originality, or they sounded like they were still in training. Chalk it up to jazz education's growing pains.

Some jazz people lamented this shift. But in college programs as in the big bands, musicians still share ideas with and test themselves against their peers, learn to blend in ensemble settings, and get practical advice about the art and business of jazz from working musicians who got their lessons the hard way. And the best students still build on what they've learned to develop their own styles.

Why did so many musicians look to the past in the 1980s?

It wasn't just Wynton Marsalis. Even progressive composers either reconsidered aspects of early jazz or unwittingly recapitulated them. The bumper crop of new saxophone quartets had a precedent in the vaudeville sax choirs like the Six Brown Brothers. After 60 years on record, jazz had covered so much ground and come so far, it could be hard for musicians to see where to go next—how to extend the tradition as their idols had. But now-neglected arranging practices from the '20s and '30s offered alternatives to hard bop's strings of consecutive solos.

Looking back was easier than it had been. In the '70s, record labels that shied away from new jazz began reissuing their massive back catalogs on LP. And that was nothing compared to the flood of '80s reissues on compact discs. Sooner or later, it all came out on CD: Ellington classics, Armstrong's '50s pop sides, organ groups, fusion jams, folk jazz, swinging advertising jingles.

As soon as Thelonious Monk died in 1982, he was universally recognized as a genius, and many musicians started playing his largely ignored tunes, now found to be full of fresh challenges. This is when Monk's clotted piano harmonies and playfully stumbling gait really entered the jazz vocabulary. Even his stylistic cousin Herbie Nichols' tunes and Blue Note albums got belated attention.

All these past masterpieces and arcana were an incredible resource, but there was a catch. Younger musicians could draw on decades of accumulated wisdom, but their own CDs had to compete in the marketplace with the giants who inspired them. Diana Krall found great songs on Nat King Cole and Anita O'Day records, but she had his reputation as a piano-playing combo leader and hers as a sultry singer to live up to.

What is postmodern jazz?

In the 1980s jazz faced the classic postmodern question—Where next?—and answered it in a classic postmodern way: take everything apart and reassemble it in a new order. Juxtapose and recontextualize. It could make for some bizarre half-man, half-fly mash-ups. Harry Connick Jr. came along singing kind of like Frank Sinatra and playing piano kind of like Monk.

Other borrowers better integrated diverse strains. Tenor saxophonist David Murray, like Albert Ayler, had played in church as a boy. On Murray's first mid-'70s recordings Ayler's influence was plain on his wide vibrato and simple, catchy melodies such as "Flowers for Albert." But soon other influences submerged that one: swing tenor Ben Webster's big bearish tone, rhythmic swagger, and stage-whispering on ballads; Eric Dolphy's way of careening from the bottom to the top of a horn's range, in big staccato leaps. Murray was jazz's most notable bass clarinetist after Dolphy, with a sweetly woody, almost bubbly sound; he'd pop notes from the mouthpiece like a vaudeville novelty clarinetist. And he synthesized it all into a personal style.

Murray played in the World Saxophone Quartet, and led numerous groups including a way-too-loose big band and a fine octet. Versatile midsize bands like that one were an '80s trend. Composer Henry Threadgill had his Sextett, in fact consisting of seven players. (He counted its two drummers as one.) With cornet or trumpet, trombone, Threadgill's reeds, cello and bass, the group could play the role of a small jazz combo, a blues band (with Diedre Murray's spiky plucked cello as guitar), cross-riffing big band or marching unit. Threadgill had served in the Army and, like fellow vets Ayler and Anthony Braxton, had a lingering affection for parade music.

The Threadgill Sextett's "Spotted Dick Is Pudding" (1987) is retro with a twist. The catchy barnyard melody Frank Lacy growls and blares on slide trombone over simple chords could predate the Civil War. It's all very unlike bop—Lacy's solo sticks close to the tune—but the tune frequently changes key by giant steps of a major third, an odd disruption that erases a sense of a home key. Hinting at ragtime's multiple themes, there's a prearranged double-time section, with horns playing preset riffs behind Threadgill's scalding alto.

Clarinetist John Carter's octets, heard on five albums in his undervalued series *Roots and Folklore: Episodes in the Development of American Folk Music*, sketches a people's diaspora from Africa through the Middle Passage to the Great Migration in a musical parallel to Alex Haley's book (and the TV miniseries) *Roots*. Carter came from Fort Worth—he was Ornette Coleman's schoolmate and Julius Hemphill's teacher—and takes venerable call-and-response traditions as a jumping-off point. His melodies smack of field hollers and country blues. But like Ellington he reimagines musical particulars: *Roots and Folklore* is his *Black, Brown, and Beige.*

Carter uses early jazz instruments—cornet, clarinet, trombone, violin, bass, and drums—but adds synthesizer, sometimes in a character role as piano or vibes. The band's woody timbres, extreme high notes, rough but transparent textures and unresolved dissonances extend the sound of Carter's clarinet. He expanded the instrument's upward range almost an octave by studying his own accidental squeaks. *Roots and Folklore* awaits a definitive edition, but a few clarinetists carry on playing his music.

Was everyone looking back?

Jazz always has its futurists. From 1985 to '93 multi-reedist Anthony Braxton's quartet with Marilyn Crispell on piano, Mark Dresser on bass, and Gerry Hemingway on drums explored novel ways to reintegrate improvisation and composition. Instead of playing a tune and then improvising away from it, they might improvise toward a written line, as if it condensed out of the blowing. They also collectively improvised transitions between compositions. At other times, bass and drums might play freestanding stop-time "pulse tracks," together or separately, while Crispell played a Braxton composition for piano and he improvised a saxophone solo over the top. On the quartet's quadruple album *Willisau (Quartet) 1991* the music has the whirling intricacy and elegance of an atom.

Dutch composer Misha Mengelberg's ICP Orchestra could work along similar lines, but Mengelberg prized the possibility of chaos. Braxton sought higher order, to prepare listeners for a world in which we're bombarded by multiple information streams all the time. Yet the conflicting layers in his music also recalled Charles Ives re-creating the sound of brass bands clashing in a town square—an earlier kind of real-world simultaneity.

Composer and pianist Anthony Davis's music was likewise new and old. It bore obvious kinship to classical composer Steve Reich's so-called minimalism, with its own roots in West Africa's overlapping rhythm cycles and the metallic sheen of Indonesian gamelan orchestras. Davis's band of eight or nine players, Episteme, played looping, overlapping phrases of varying lengths: 11/4 piano versus 7/4 marimba on "Wayang No. 2 (Shadowdance)." There was a lot of that loop-and-overlap in the '80s. As usual there was a precedent. For his mid-1950s piece "Turkish Mambo," Lennie Tristano multitracked three pianos in different time signatures, an ivory and ebony drum choir.

What did Miles Davis do in the '80s? What else was happening in electric jazz?

Davis stopped performing in the mid-'70s, and his early-'80s return was eagerly awaited. He now played for bigger crowds, but his best music was behind him. His loud septets and octets offered arena-size gestures: long guitar solos, splashy keyboard chords, synthesized strings, and deep-pocket funk grooves with little variation. Even with good players like guitarist John Scofield and saxophonists Kenny Garrett and Gary Thomas passing through, his bands lacked the jittery agitation of his '70s funk.

Davis had always looked to his musicians and arrangers for good ideas, but the aides he now relied on were record producers; he'd sometimes dub solos onto prerecorded tracks. His diminished involvement was partly due to health woes. He sometimes evoked his old lyricism, economy, and plaintive tone on such pop tunes as Cyndi Lauper's "Time after Time" and Michael Jackson's "Human Nature," but there were fewer opportunities for him to play his old role as band catalyst and editor.

Ornette Coleman continued on with his electric Prime Time. Some of its alumni formed their own forward-/backward-looking bands. Drummer Ronald Shannon Jackson, also from Fort Worth and a veteran of Albert Ayler and Cecil Taylor groups, had his Decoding Society. Like Ayler, he featured inspirational marchlike themes. As in Prime Time, each player might paraphrase or embroider a rhythm or melodic phrase in a different way or different key. And a piece might unfold in several layers of rhythm, as Taylor's music does.

Ronald Shannon Jackson's 1982 "Iola" is very different from but as intricately layered as an Anthony Davis composition. There are repeating loops of material for each rhythm instrument including two electric basses and banjo, while three horns play a long-note melody that works variations on similar phrases, and Jackson's drums cross a march with New Orleans funk. Most of the melodic material is derived from a major scale, but solos may wander from the home key, in the manner of Ornette Coleman. It's more new music made from old parts.

What about guitarists? James Blood Ulmer? Pat Metheny? John Scofield? Bill Frisell?

Ronald Shannon Jackson sometimes collaborated with the similarly modern/retro James Blood Ulmer, who had been an Ornette Coleman protégé in the '70s. Ulmer's thwacked-chord guitar playing and the interplay between his axe and mumbled vocals updated 1920s country blues. The offbeat syncopation of "Swing & Things" for a guitar, drums, and electric violin trio echoes 1950s rockabilly, but at the end of every chorus there's a tricky, stop-time turnaround out of 1970s fusion. The juxtapositions of country blues, rockabilly, and electric jazz don't sound incongruous; they give Ulmer's music a timeless feel.

Missouri-born Pat Metheny's harmonies are informed by pop and Brazilian music, and his bands can be heartland-sunny. But he also has a strong affinity for Ornette Coleman's music, displayed on the album 80/81 with Coleman and Keith Jarrett alums Charlie Haden on bass and Dewey Redman on tenor, alongside saxophonist Michael Brecker, a master of post-Coltrane shellacked tone and chord-and-scale higher math. The guitarist also led a trio with Haden and Coleman's old drummer Billy Higgins before Metheny and Coleman collaborated on 1985's dense and bracing *Song X*, in which saxophone and guitar synthesizer swarm like bees.

Before joining Miles Davis in the '80s, John Scofield had already made his reputation as a fusion and mainstream picker with pronounced bluesy inflections. Some guitarists have one groove they gravitate to. Scofield had a few: straight swing feel, swing feel with a country twist, New Orleans R&B mambo, deep blues, heavy funk. Like Metheny or Bill Frisell, and unlike many '70s fusion musicians, he rarely overplayed, leaving spaces and breath pauses in his lines.

Traditional jazz guitarists favor a pick-heavy attack to articulate swing; it's all about the precise timing of the front of the note. Bill Frisell went the other way. He used volume pedal to fade in a note after he picked it, so the sound swelled up from silence, and he made frequent use of a string-bending, note-bending "whammy bar." Those swells and bends made him sound oddly like a Nashville pedal-steel guitarist and gave his urbane playing a rural twang. But he was also a keen student of Thelonious Monk's unorthodox ways of accompanying fellow musicians.

Like Scofield and Metheny, Frisell dug rock guitar's ringing sustain and post-Hendrix distortion. Frisell's gizmos included delay units to let him loop and repeat phrases and layer them over each other—a radical variation on minimalism's polyrhythmic loops. Flawless timing helped. Live, he'd line up the overlapping parts with uncanny precision.

Drummer Paul Motian tapped Frisell for a quintet and trio with tenor saxophonist Joe Lovano, who'd absorbed his Coleman (the rangy blues feeling) and Coltrane (a strong sound in all registers). But Lovano's plaintive quality was his own, and it gave exquisite feeling to ballads.

The Motian-Frisell-Lovano trio helped popularize bands without bass players: bassless became the new pianoless. The trio kept the familiar theme-solos-theme format, but everything else was Dali's melting watch. Frisell's string-bending chords seemed to slide in and out of tune, without conflicting with Lovano's harmonically oriented lines. While most drummers aim to keep a steady pulse, Motian speeded up and slowed down in conversation with guitar and saxophone. They played tunes by Motian, Monk, Billie Holiday, and Motian's old boss Bill Evans. As clearly as any group of the 1980s, '90s, or early 2000s, the trio demonstrated how old and new players, compositions, and ideas could all get along.

What is "M-base"? How did electric saxophone make a comeback?

Around 1984, some younger New York musicians banded together in the loose confederation known as M-base, short for Macro-Basic Array of Structured Extemporizations. That name didn't give much away, but the collective attracted attention from the press and record labels. Generally, M-basers expressed a desire to push jazz language forward, drawing on the rhythmic energy of funk, hip-hop, and West African music.

They were stylistically diverse. Cassandra Wilson was a sultry singer of originals and standards, influenced by Abbey Lincoln and Betty Carter. Pianist Geri Allen primarily recorded in traditional trios with bass and drums. In the mid-'90s, she became one of Ornette Coleman's rare pianists, in an acoustic quartet.

The movement's driving forces were alto saxophonists Steve Coleman and Greg Osby, who developed a slippery approach to harmony, played modern electric funk, and explored digital updates of Eddie Harris's electric saxophone technology. They weren't the only ones doing that. Soprano saxophonist Jane Ira Bloom used electronic boosters, triggered by motion and velocity sensors that exploited her tendency to swing the bell of her horn around while playing. Michael Brecker occasionally played an Electronic Wind Instrument (EWI), a synthesizer with saxophone-like fingering and breath control.

Steve Coleman was yet another '80s musician inspired by West African rhythm systems, assigning different musicians looping phrases of different duration, to generate ever-shifting combinations of accents. James Brown's superheated funk was another inspiration for its micromanaged short note values. But Coleman kept a cool head as an improviser and composer. The basic form of his 1985 "Wights Waits for Weights" is 8 bars of 3/4, followed by a pause of one extra beat before the next chorus: a hiccup. He recorded it under his own name, and as part of a fine quintet run by bassist Dave Holland, who was also fascinated by long and overlapping rhythm cycles.

Coming up in Chicago, Coleman had absorbed how saxophonists Bunky Green and Von Freeman would improvise sequences far removed from a tune's key—possibly using a scale or mode sharing only a note or two with the home scale. So would James Brown's saxophonist Maceo Parker, who had his own cool, detached tone. Coleman played in all manner of acoustic and electric settings, teaming up at times with Branford Marsalis and mixing M-basers with such elders as Freeman and English trumpeter Kenny Wheeler.

In the '80s, some observers dismissed M-base as all hype, but Coleman and Osby influenced dozens of younger players.

How did cartoon music influence postmodern jazz?
What are "game pieces"?

Baby boomers had been exposed to postmodern juxtapositions all their lives, via 1940s and '50s Warner Bros. cartoons, staples of children's TV. Tracking Bugs Bunny's antics scene by scene and shot by shot, Carl Stalling's cartoon music was a riot of quick cuts or abrupt transitions from one mood, tempo, texture, and genre to another, fortified with inside-joke quotes from pop songs, European classics, bugle calls, and patriotic anthems—the same jumble of far-flung melodies that jazz soloists quote from. Stalling said his scores mimicked how he used to accompany silent films in theaters, sometimes improvising, sometimes falling back on stock motifs.

In the '80s and '90s Stalling was championed by alto saxophonist and composer John Zorn, whose own pieces reflected the same disjunctive aesthetic, sometimes characterized as "channel zapping" by analogy with impatient viewers watching TV with a thumb on the remote control.

Zorn devised quick-cut pieces for improvisers—for example, his 25-minute *Spillane* (1986), as in crime novelist Mickey Spillane, for nine players including guitarist Bill Frisell, two keyboardists, and a harpist. Its episodic sections played with the conventions of radio drama and Hollywood crime stories—mumbled tough-guy voiceovers, panicky screams, and barking dogs, the sounds of a prizefight, bump-and-grind strip-club music, roadhouse blues, and windshield wipers in the rain. There were snippets of hard bop and Nelson Riddle's TV theme *Route 66*. Zorn didn't write much of it out. Mostly he described the effect he sought, and let the players work out solutions. Episodes were recorded individually, in sequence. Postmodern improvisers had inspired postmodern composing: if musicians could play in all sorts of styles, why not do it all in one place?

Zorn also wrote game pieces for improvisers, with elaborate rules, hand signals, and cue cards. The basic idea was one that classical composers including Mauricio Kagel and Zorn's friend Misha Mengelberg had toyed with in the 1960s. Zorn's most elegant and popular game was "Cobra," in which Stalling's quick-cut aesthetic is built in. Musicians might be called on to make radical changes on cue or to deliberately clash with other players. A prompter/conductor acts as traffic cop, fielding signaled requests from the musicians. The object of the game is to create a piece of music in real time.

What is conducted improvising?

The idea of a leader or conductor shaping a piece of music while it's being performed is an old one; every big bandleader who ever pointed at someone to solicit a solo did that. In the 1920s, King Oliver and Louis Armstrong dazzled audiences with coherent two-cornet breaks. A few bars beforehand, Oliver would silently finger the valves of his horn to give Armstrong some idea what he'd play on the next break.

By the 1960s, Sun Ra helped shape his Arkestra's collective improvisations using cues and tracing lines in the air. Later, such leaders as Muhal Richard Abrams, Charles Moffett, Misha Mengelberg, Roscoe Mitchell, and George Lewis similarly conducted improvisers, often using informal pantomime.

In the 1980s, cornetist Butch Morris made a specialty of what he called "conduction," using a repertoire of dozens of specific cues he'd rehearse with musicians. He conducted his own groups, David Murray's big band, bassist Maarten Altena's Dutch ensemble, groups of jazz or classical players, and musicians from Turkey.

What was the "downtown scene"?

In the '80s and '90s, New York's so-called downtown musicians were primarily showcased at venues in Lower Manhattan, although many lived elsewhere. The scene's unofficial clubhouse from 1987 to '94 was the original Knitting Factory on Houston Street. The scene was actually a loose set of overlapping subscenes: M-base musicians; John Zorn and his allies; baby boom and post-boom improvisers coming more out of rock than jazz; players whose development started in the 1970s avant-garde, such as alto saxophonists Tim Berne and Marty Ehrlich; bop refugees drawn to more open concepts, such as ex–Horace Silver trumpeter Dave Douglas; veteran free jazz musicians now working with younger players, including bassists Reggie Workman (who'd played with John Coltrane) and William Parker (from Cecil Taylor's unit) and tenor saxophonists Charles Gayle and David S. Ware.

Do all the great jazz musicians live in New York?

New York City's the jazz capital, with more talented players and places to play than anywhere else, from short-lived venues to venerable clubs like the Village Vanguard and the Blue Note, to modern-day institutions such as Smalls, Jazz Standard, and Iridium. Moving to New York is a dream and rite of passage for countless musicians. But Boston, Chicago, Los Angeles, Vancouver, Paris, Tokyo, and many other cities have their share of fine players, and others live out in the country or teach in college towns. Such outliers may escape New Yorkers' attention, however. It took the lyrical, powerful, subtle saxophonist/cornetist/valve trombonist Joe McPhee decades to get his due in New York, living as he did 70 miles upriver in Poughkeepsie, long after he became a regular in Europe.

What were the early '90s "jazz wars" about?

In 1991, Wynton Marsalis was named director of the new jazz department at the New York arts complex Lincoln Center, and naturally enough programmed music that reflected his own tastes. He ignored what was still called the avant-garde, but it's not like Lincoln Center's classical-music programs were in the vanguard either. The object was to fill seats.

Still, Marsalis and his allies insisted that Jazz at Lincoln Center represented every phase of jazz and, when asked, explained that excluded musicians such as Cecil Taylor and Anthony Braxton were not part of jazz at all. This small-tent revisionism led to endless squabbling in print and in clubs among musicians, critics, and fans. Intemperate accusations were exchanged. Sinister racial motives were attributed to the African American Marsalis for failing to celebrate Bix Beiderbecke and to white critics who questioned Marsalis's programming. (Disclosure: I was among them.) Marsalis and Cecil Taylor were both accused of sounding too much like classical musicians. Marsalis, who occasionally performed classics, was said to play jazz without feeling; Taylor supposedly cribbed from Messiaen. Some jazz people outside New York, by the way, thought the whole controversy was a local story that got way too much attention.

And yet, musicians from allegedly opposing camps were writing music that had much in common. "Hustle Bustle" from a Marsalis dance suite quickly rummaged through different styles in a postmodern way. So did the extended blues "Bloodline," by AACM founder Muhal Richard Abrams's terrific New York big band, which collapsed together decades of styles starting with the 1920s. Muhal's orchestra reflected the full breadth of the big band tradition, mixing classic swing and free improvisation, rather like Sun Ra's Arkestra.

Marsalis and company criticized Anthony Braxton for blurring jazz and contemporary classical music. But in the '90s, Marsalis himself mixed high-art and vernacular styles in the string quartet "At the Octoroon Balls" and "A Fiddler's Tale Suite" for chamber septet.

Wynton's views got wide exposure in Ken Burns's marathon PBS series *Jazz* of 2001, which barely glanced at music after 1960 (except to celebrate Marsalis's arrival to save jazz from extinction) and in which the only musician who takes a real drubbing is Cecil Taylor.

That battle was won, but in the end the war was lost. Braxton and Taylor still got booked at jazz clubs and festivals and reviewed in jazz magazines. In time Jazz at Lincoln Center booked Dutch anarchists Misha Mengelberg and Han Bennink, John Zorn, and even Taylor himself.

Didn't Anthony Braxton himself say he wasn't a jazz musician?

Yes, for the same reason Duke Ellington did in the 1940s, when critics like John Hammond advised him to stick to dance music and forgo ambitious suites like *Black, Brown, and Beige*: to sidestep criticism that such music was outside jazz's purview. One of Duke's highest compliments was to declare a musician "beyond category." But that didn't stop him from headlining jazz festivals and writing tunes with "jazz" in the title, and it didn't stop Lincoln Center from programming his music. It also didn't stop Braxton from improvising on Monk, Charlie Parker, and Andrew Hill tunes with a rhythm section.

What was the relationship between American jazz and world music after 1990?

Jazz continued its long habit of soaking up international rhythms, abetted by a general boom of interest in global musics, on CDs especially. New York's downtown scene embraced Balkan rhythms. Musicians were playing 5-beat patterns as though it were 1959 all over again, except that a Balkan 5/8, as on "Red Emma," by Dave Douglas's trumpet-guitar-drums Tiny Bell Trio, was quicker and had more of the air of a European folk dance than Brubeck's 5/4 did.

There was renewed intermingling between New York's jazz and Latin musicians. Henry Threadgill hired tubist Edwin Rodriguez from the Fania All-Stars for his two-tuba septet Very Very Circus. Puerto Rican pianist Edsel Gomez played with clarinetist Don Byron, who also played klezmer music. Like Balkan, that downtown fad had roots in players' student days at Boston music schools.

Many modern musicians are record collectors with diverse interests that influence their jazz. Saxophonist and clarinetist Michael Moore wrote pieces inspired by music from the Croatian island of Krk and arranged a tune from Madagascar. Dave Douglas transcribed, for quintet, a fast, rhythmically tricky traditional melody from Burma.

Speech rhythms had influenced jazz since 1920s brass players picked up plunger mutes. Now saxophonist Greg Osby walked around New York's ethnic neighborhoods, soaking up non-English speech cadences he'd imitate on his horn. Pianist Jason Moran, who'd passed through Osby's band, wrote "Ringing My Phone (Straight Outta Istanbul)" whose contours and rhythms shadowed one end of a Turkish phone call.

Starting in the late '90s, jazz turned again to music of India. Henry Threadgill and pianist Myra Melford spent time there. Melford began playing harmonium—played with one hand, its bellows pumped with the other—which she'd studied with Indian masters. Indian American pianist Vijay Iyer spun long, involuted lines full of complex rhythms, owing something to '70s fusion music with its own Indian-American syntheses, and to early employer Steve Coleman's intricate beats. Rudresh Mahanthappa, one of numerous altoists influenced by Coleman, confronted his cultural roots directly on the 2007 recording *Kinsmen* with Indian classical saxophonist Kadri Gopalnath and a mixed Indian and American band that mediated between riffing Americana and Carnatic microtonal intervals without papering over their differences.

Is jazz influenced by East Asian musics? What about Asian American musicians?

Chinese and Japanese musics have their own wind, string, and percussion ensembles, and they use pentatonic scales much like West Africa's. East Asian instrumentalists cultivate striking timbres, employ expressive vibrato and tremolo, and bend pitches in speechlike or birdlike ways, so there's plenty of common ground to explore. In the '90s, bassist Anthony Brown's Asian American Orchestra played Monk tunes with Steve Lacy, and the Ellington-Strayhorn *Far East Suite* using Asian instruments. California's Miya Masaoka played Monk on Japanese koto, with bass and drums.

They weren't the first to go pan-Pacific. In the '70s, Toshiko Akiyoshi, who'd played bebop piano in Japan before settling in the United States in the 1950s, began writing for her own jazz orchestras. She'd sometimes swing traditional Japanese melodies, and she used tsuzumi hourglass drums on her 1976 suite "Minamata." Akiyoshi wrote frequently for massed flutes. The co-leader of her first big band, tenor saxophonist Lew Tabackin, played flute and piccolo with a pure, piercing tone, bending notes in a shakuhachi-inspired way on "Sumie" that same year.

In the '80s, a wave of politically engaged Asian American leaders emerged. San Francisco pianist Jon Jang's Pan-Asian Arkestra mixed Chinese and western flutes, jazz horns, Asian double-reeds, and erhu fiddle, for some bracing, singular blends. His 1991 "Concerto for Jazz Ensemble and Taiko" juxtaposed Japanese taiko drums, West African talking drum and American trap set, rather like Max Roach mixing American, West African and Caribbean percussion on his 1960 *Freedom Now Suite*. At one moment in "Great Wall/Gold Mountain" from Jang's *Tiananmen!* suite for mixed ensemble, an Ellingtonian train song, the chugging staccato chords of a sheng (mouth organ), and a Coplandesque cowboy melody collide. Anyone who knows who laid train tracks through the American West gets the point immediately: it's cultural history as witty pictogram.

Are there Native American jazz musicians?

Many jazz musicians have Native American ancestry including Frank Trumbauer, John Lewis, Dave Brubeck, Sunny Murray, Cecil Taylor, and singers Mildred Bailey, Lee Wiley, and Kay Starr, but they have seldom dealt with that heritage explicitly.

Kaw-Creek tenor saxophonist Jim Pepper, who'd played in Paul Motian's '80s quintet with Bill Frisell and Joe Lovano, wrote some compositions based on Native American chanting, including "Dakota Song" and the 1969 Brewer & Shipley pop hit "Witchi-Tai-To." Pepper chants a bit on his own version of the latter.

The jazz master of that practice is bop singer Sheila Jordan, inspired by her Cherokee grandfather. Jordan uses chanting to ease her way into a couple of versions of the Beatles' "Blackbird" and to improvise over a modal backdrop on her 1999 version of Steve Kuhn's "The Zoo." She connects jazz scat singing to a much older tradition of rhythmic, syllabic vocalizing.

How did hip-hop affect jazz?

The drum, organ, or guitar licks sampled and looped on '80s hip-hop records typically came from vintage and sometimes obscure hard bop/soul jazz LPs, prompting reissues of same on CD. In the late '80s and early '90s, when hip-hop was pop, some jazz musicians tried rapping themselves, faddishly (bop trumpeters Red Rodney and Jon Faddis), or they hired rappers or deejays for special projects (Branford Marsalis, Greg Osby, Cassandra Wilson), without making much of a dent in either jazz or hip-hop.

Hip-hop's sampled, looped inflexible drum patterns were an awkward fit with jazz's flexible pulse and dynamics. It took awhile before jazz drummers got beyond quoting hip-hop beats for effect and started to integrate those beats into their rhythmic vocabularies.

The rhythms of syncopated rapping also found their way into jazz. Saxophonist Greg Osby is partial to beat patterns that, like a rapper's, shuttle accents between up and down beats, as on 1988's "Chin Lang." Electronics both hinder and help here: Rodney Green triggers fat but dynamically flat snare drum samples, while a gizmo shadowing Osby's alto adds a percussive snap to every note, a sound like flipping book pages. On "Concepticus in C" a decade later, the sometimes narrow melodic range of Osby's alto line makes the rap connection more obvious, and Green's work on a conventional drum kit breathes more freely. It's as rhythmically complex as '70s fusion, but it swings more.

The organist on "Concepticus," Jason Moran, usually plays piano. He made jazz-hip-hop connections explicit by recording a multitracked solo piano transcription of Afrika Bambaata's rap classic "Planet Rock." Moran prepared his piano by laying paper over the strings, clipping small objects to or wedging objects between them, for a more percussive sound. While working on that adaptation, he came up with a new bass line he spun off into "Planet Rock Postscript," which is even further removed from its source. So do new ideas develop from old ones. The album they appeared on, *Modernistic*, also featured Moran's modernized take on James P. Johnson's 1929 "You've Got to Be Modernistic."

How did jazz respond to pop in the '90s and first decade of the 2000s?

In the '90s, as in the '60s, jazz musicians tapped the post-Beatles rock and pop repertoire. Guitarist Bill Frisell played John Hiatt and Madonna tunes on 1993's *Have a Little Faith*, alongside music by Stephen Foster, Sousa,

Ives, Copland, Sonny Rollins, Muddy Waters, and Bob Dylan: Americana broadly conceived. In the '90s Frisell also began exploring country music. Singers likewise picked up on contemporary or at least post-Beatles pop. Cassandra Wilson did the Monkees' "Last Train to Clarksville," and songs by Joni Mitchell, Van Morrison, Neil Young, and U2. A version of bluesman Muddy Waters' "Honey Bee" on 2003's *Glamoured* suggested a source for her increasingly languorous vocal style, and drew a connection to her Mississippi roots.

One significant trend since 2000 was the rebirth of the venerable piano-bass-drums combo as a new kind of power trio, a trend anticipated in the 1990s by Medeski, Martin, and Wood, who deployed club-conscious rhythms even before John Medeski swapped piano for organ and the band started playing rock clubs.

The breakthrough twenty-first-century power trio was the Bad Plus, in which resourceful jazz pianist Ethan Iverson indulged a newfound love of rocking out. They played Nirvana's "Smells Like Teen Spirit" and Abba's "Knowing Me, Knowing You," an oddball repertoire not unlike Sonny Rollins playing Dolly Parton's "Here You Come Again." They play the tunes because they like them, but the apparent absurdity doesn't hurt.

Jason Moran had the Bandwagon, his jazz trio made over when Tarus Mateen switched from upright bass to big-bodied bass guitar. Vijay Iyer played in the alto-piano-drums Fieldwork, in which drummer Elliot Kavee played loopy but breathing hip-hop-derived beats and hiccuping rhythm patterns. Swedish trio E.S.T. was heavily hyped for accessible dance rhythms descended from Detroit techno and English drum-and-bass grooves.

What are the "new standards"?

Herbie Hancock's 1996 album *The New Standard* featured jazzed-up versions of Nirvana's "All Apologies," Billy Joel's "New York Minute," and songs by Peter Gabriel, Prince, and Sade. Hancock may have intended that title to be a little joke, but the name stuck, and "new standard" was then applied to any post-Beatles pop tune covered by a jazz instrumentalist or singer.

The term was a misnomer, based on a misunderstanding of what a standard is. Standards aren't tunes borrowed from pop, although the majority of jazz standards came from the Broadway-Hollywood songbook, but songs that are part of the common repertoire. Standards are tunes you could request at a jam session or play with an unfamiliar rhythm section—tunes, in short, that jazz musicians perform regularly. By that measure, just about no "new standard" is a real standard. The Beatles' "Blackbird," with its lovely melody and roving chords, has been covered by dozens of jazz artists, including singers Nina Simone, Sarah Vaughan, and Sheila Jordan, pianists Brad Mehldau and Uri Caine, and drummer Tony Williams's quintet. But it's rarely heard at jam sessions.

Brad Mehldau, a fine ballad player evoking Bill Evans's sensitive touch and Keith Jarrett's expansive romanticism, treats Nick Drake's "River Man" and Radiohead's "Paranoid Android" and "Exit Music (For a Film)" as personal standards, recording them in multiple settings. That shows a serious commitment to developing new repertoire.

Is the current era more congenial to jazzwomen?

Just as the second women's movement of the '60s and '70s created opportunities throughout the culture, so too in jazz as part of that culture, not least by prompting men to examine their prejudices. Besides the female instrumentalists mentioned elsewhere in this chapter, their contemporaries include pianists Michelle Rosewoman and Renee Rosnes, singer and pianist Patricia Barber, drummers Teri Lyne Carrington, Cindy Blackman, Susie Ibarra, and Allison Miller, trumpeter

Ingrid Jensen, trombonist Deborah Weisz, saxophonist Virginia May-hew, clarinetist Anat Cohen, flutists Nicole Mitchell and Ali Ryerson, guitarist Mary Halvorson, and cellists Peggy Lee and Tomeka Reid—a far from definitive list, cutting across various styles. One of New York's premier big bands is led by composer Maria Schneider, who apprenticed with Gil Evans.

There was also a resurgence of jazz/adult pop singers in the '90s and 2000s, including high-profile Cassandra Wilson, Jane Monheit, and pianist Diana Krall. There were male vocalists too, including Sinatra-inspired Harry Connick, Connick-inspired Michael Bublé, and ballad and scat singer Kurt Elling.

Is there still an avant-garde in jazz?

Musicians still come up with new ideas, but listeners aren't as easy to shock as they once were. Free jazz has continued to thrive, and though some fans insist it's still avant-garde or "cutting edge," in reality it's one more historical style musicians play in updated form, whose basic parameters were laid out decades ago, like dixieland or hard bop.

Not that there's anything wrong with that. The true test of musicians in any style is how well they play it. Free jazz tenor saxophonist Charles Gayle's '90s work wouldn't have sounded out of place in 1966, but he could really play.

In 2002, tenor saxophonist David S. Ware recorded a version of Sonny Rollins's 1958 *Freedom Suite*—as did Branford Marsalis the year before, alongside a version of John Coltrane's 1964 album-length suite *A Love Supreme*. Branford had been leading his own bands from the mid-'80s and had grown into a formidable tenor saxophonist. In his playing, one hears traces of Coltrane's rippling scales and soaring high notes, but they've become part of his own expressive arsenal. Jazz musicians revisit such classics much the way classical musicians play

Bach on modern instruments, honoring the masterworks in the terms of one's own time. Practitioners of any historical jazz style usually incorporate later refinements, by design or through inadvertent anachronisms. They play living music, not museum pieces.

One great free jazz group in the new century was bassist William Parker's quartet with Rob Brown on alto and Lewis Barnes on trumpet. Parker had already partnered in other bands with its powerhouse drummer Hamid Drake, who brought a wealth of experience playing reggae and other global musics as well as free jazz. Parker and Drake juggle multiple rhythms without throwing each other. Their deep grooves when they pull together smack of Jamaican dub music or North African frame-drum beats more than the Albert Ayler trio's free timing.

What were new developments in bop? Did free improvisation finally become mainstream?

Some younger bop musicians in the '90s and 2000s looked at old schools from new perspectives, investigating musicians who didn't get their due in their own time. Tenor saxophonist Mark Turner drew on the legacy of the ultra-cool Warne Marsh. Pianists Frank Kimbrough, Geri Allen, Ethan Iverson, and Ted Rosenthal played music of '50s composer Herbie Nichols, as had Roswell Rudd, Misha Mengelberg, and bassist Buell Neidlinger before them. Allen and Dave Douglas played music by Mary Lou Williams.

By the early twenty-first century, old stylistic divisions had broken down. Young lions had gone electric, and free improvisation had been absorbed into the poly-stylism of jazz at large, part of a well-rounded player's menu of strategies.

Nobody was as effortlessly polyglot as alto saxophonist Lee Konitz. A half century after his debut with Claude Thornhill, he had a tone as pliant and plaintive and a mind as fertile as ever. Konitz sounded at home fronting bop rhythm sections all over the world (finding fresh routes through tunes he'd played forever), sitting in and recording with the quirky Paul Motian–Bill Frisell–Joe Lovano trio, and free improvising with Derek Bailey and company in England. But then he'd been playing bop, free music, and the long game since he was with Lennie Tristano in the 1940s.

In the '80s, pianist Keith Jarrett formed a long-running trio with bassist Gary Peacock—now as lyrical as he was manic with Albert Ayler—and polyrhythmic drummer Jack DeJohnette, a Jarrett ally since the '60s. The trio played only standards or free improvisations; the free stuff might recall Ornette Coleman's friskiness or the slow, rubato, droning quality of North Indian classical music. Trumpeter Dave Ballou's 2000 album *On This Day* was free improvised, but his quintet played melodies, harmonized, took solos in order, changed up the rhythms, traded phrases, and ended together as if it had been scripted, all with a fine sense of balance and proportion.

On the duo recital *Freefall* (2000), bop pianist Kenny Barron and postmodern violinist Regina Carter played standards, including an ingeniously intricate recasting of Thelonious Monk's blues "Misterioso" in which they bounced the skeletal melody back and forth in various pre-plotted ways, their syncopations updating ragtime. The title track was an improvisation where they riffled through a lexicon of free players' pet devices: mirrorlike imitation, leapfrogging trades and cat-and-mouse chases, fast transitions, staccato notes scattered around for a little musical pointillism, and moments when they pretend to ignore each other.

In our time, leaders such as Dave Douglas, Don Byron, and John Zorn lead multiple acoustic or electric bands to scratch different itches. Musicians' options are wider nowadays partly because their training is.

In 1999, the jazz, classical, klezmer, Latin, and gospel pianist Uri Caine revamped J. S. Bach's 1742 *Goldberg Variations*. Bach had spun his 30 variations off a basic form and chord sequence. Caine arranged all of those and added 40 more, approaching the material from all over the Western musical map. There were Colombian, techno, and gospel variations; settings for modern and period string quartets; weird mixes of baroque and free players; Bach in the styles of Mozart, Alban Berg, dixieland, modern bop, and Wendy Carlos on Moog synthesizer. It was spectacularly wide-ranging, with the supple jazz variations part of a larger whole.

With seemingly everyone referencing the past some kind of way, is jazz's development over?

It may look that way sometimes, from a twenty-first-century perspective. But so far all end-of-history arguments have turned out to be wrong. Consider the words of the observer who wrote, "Theatrical music in Spain is today so advanced and so highly developed in all its aspects, that it seems impossible it could go any further."[4] That was in 1689.

Jazz from the beginning was a hybrid music, susceptible to influences from several continents. As the world shrinks, more cultures come into play. There is plenty of room to grow. And jazz has always shown a capacity to reinvent itself out of its own root materials.

What is the future of jazz?

Nobody knows. Critics' predictions of where jazz is going are usually well off the mark, because we don't know what—or who—may be just around the corner.

Glossary

AABA form The typical form for a classic 32-bar pop song, divided into four 8-bar sections. The main melody is sung or played twice, sometimes with slight variations the second time, followed by a contrasting B section—the **bridge**—before a repeat of the main theme.

additive rhythm A complex rhythm pattern made by combining simpler units, usually of 2 or 3 beats; for instance, the 2+2+2+3 9-beat rhythm pattern of Dave Brubeck's "Blue Rondo à la Turk."

alternate take A recorded version of a tune not originally selected for release; compare **master take**.

antiphony See **call-and-response**.

arrangement An orchestration or reorchestration tailored for a specific instrumentation or collection of players.

backbeat A heavy accent on beats 2 and 4 of a 4-beat bar.

bar A unit of musical time that identifies a piece's basic recurring rhythm or metrical pattern, set off by vertical bars on sheet music. A bar in 3/4 time is the length of three quarter notes, for example.

Bird Nickname for Charlie Parker.

blowing Improvising, not necessarily on a wind instrument.

breaks Moments in a performance when most instruments in a band drop out for 1 or 2 bars, to let a solo instrument (or two) perform unaccompanied.

bridge The secondary theme in a jazz or pop tune.

call-and-response A dialogue between solo and/or massed voices, often with variable "calls" answered by a fixed refrain. Also known as **antiphony**.

chart A written arrangement.

chops Technical abilities.

chords Any combination of three or more notes that, when sounded together, Western listeners hear as one sound.

chorus One cycle through the form of a tune.

chromatic scale All 12 notes contained within an octave: for example, on a piano, all the white and black keys between one C and the next.

cluster or **tone cluster** At least three adjacent notes of a scale (or on a keyboard), sounded simultaneously, for a dense and cloudlike sound.

comping The act of accompanying a soloist on a instrument capable of playing chords, such as piano or guitar.

contrafact A new melody that fits the chords of an existing song.

counterpoint The art of juxtaposing two or more independent melody lines, which are related to each other or the underlying chords harmonically.

dynamics Degrees of loudness and softness; fluctuations in volume.

field holler An agricultural worker's stylized solo shout, related to a collective **work song.**

head arrangement An arrangement created in rehearsal with input from the members of the band, which might not be written down.

lick A favorite musical phrase an improviser will insert into a solo, sometimes for want of a better alternative.

master take When several performances of a piece are recorded during a session, the one originally released is the master, as opposed to an **alternate take.**

minstrelsy The dominant form of entertainment in the United States during the mid-nineteenth century, in which whites in blackface makeup parodied black songs and body language in satirical or sentimental sketches. In time, African American minstrels in blackface would parody whites' poorly observed imitations.

modal jazz Narrowly, jazz in which players improvise using the notes found in **modes,** rather than underlying chords; broadly, jazz in which the chords change infrequently.

modes A set of seven notes, drawn from the chromatic scale. The Ionian mode is the same as a major scale; Dorian mode resembles a minor scale. Other common modes include the Lydian, Phrygian, and Mixolydian.

mute An object placed in or over the bell of a brass instrument like trumpet or trombone, which alters the tone of the instrument. The mute might be fixed in place or manipulated by the player.

nonet A nine-piece band.

odd meters Any music in which the number of beats per bar is in an odd number greater than three. As jazz musicians apply the term, a 3-beat waltz doesn't count.

offbeats The beats between the main beats of a bar: the *ands* when you're counting "1 *and* 2 *and* 3 *and* 4 *and.*"

ostinato A short repeating figure, often found in the bass, and sometimes played with minor variations.

pentatonic scale A five-note series, such as the one found on a piano's black keys.

pizzicato Sounding a note on a stringed instrument by plucking (not bowing) a string.

Pres Nickname for Lester Young.

reed instrument Any instrument with a reed in the mouthpiece, such as saxophone or clarinet; more broadly, any instrument (including flute) played by a member of a band's saxophone/reed section.

Rhythm and blues (R&B) A style of African American music that evolved in the 1940s, featuring earthy, bluesy melodies and a strong underlying beat.

rhythm changes The chord sequence to George Gershwin's "I Got Rhythm."

rhythm section The instruments in a band or orchestra that define the underlying beat: usually drums, bass, and piano and/or guitar.

scat singing Improvising a sung melodic solo, using nonsense syllables.

session In jazz parlance, depending on context, this refers to either a recording session or a jam session, where musicians meet to play together informally.

soli Quasi-improvised written passages for massed horns, usually saxophones.

solo A featured, usually improvised statement by a particular instrument or musician in the course of an ensemble performance; an unaccompanied improvisation.

soundie A short film for 1940s video jukeboxes, forerunner to a music video.

standard A song or instrumental piece in the common repertoire of musicians in any musical genre, such as jazz.

stop-time rhythm The pulsing motion of sharp ensemble accents separated by short silences.

syncopation Any deviation from a regular pattern of beats in music, to make rhythms more complex and dynamic; placing a heavy accent on a normally unstressed beat in a bar.

timbre The quality of a voice or instrument's tone: smooth, rough, and so on.

trades In a band performance, a rapid sequence where each player gets a few bars (typically 4 or 2, or 4 then 2) to make a concise comment, often picking up where the last player left off. Trades typically occur toward the end of a performance.

tremolo Rapid repetitions of a single note, perceived as a continuous but pulsating sound.

triplet A group of three notes evenly divided over 1 or 2 beats.

valve trombone A trombone with three fingered valves, like a trumpet, instead of a slide.

vibrato Rapid fluctuations in pitch.

walking bass A roving bass line consisting mostly of evenly timed quarter notes, four to the bar, in 4/4 time.

work song A call-and-response melody between lead singer and the members of a work gang, used to set a tempo and coordinate labor.

Notes

Chapter 2

1. Eddie Condon with Thomas Sugrue, *We Called It Music* (1947; revised 1962; repr., New York: Da Capo, 1992), 85.

Chapter 3

1. For an excellent discussion of Monk's piano and composing techniques, see Ran Blake, "The Monk Piano Style" (1982), in Rob van der Bliek, ed., *The Thelonious Monk Reader* (New York: Oxford University Press, 2001), 248–260.

2. Sonny Rollins Trio, *The Freedom Suite* (Riverside Records RLP12–258, 1958), liner notes. Quoted in Eric Nisenson, *Open Sky: Sonny Rollins and His World of Improvisation* (New York: Da Capo, 2000), 125.

3. "Louis Armstrong, Barring Soviet Tour, Denounces Eisenhower and Gov. Faubus," *New York Times*, September 19, 1957. Quoted in

David Margolick, "The Day Louis Armstrong Made Noise," *New York Times*, September 23, 2007. Available at http://www.nytimes.com/2007/09/23/opinion/23margolick.html.

4. Dave Brubeck, *Time Out* (Columbia Records CL 1397, 1959), liner notes.

Chapter 4

1. Ekkehard Jost, *Free Jazz* (1974, repr., New York: Da Capo, 1994), 78–83.

2. Mark Gridley, *Jazz Styles: History and Analysis*, 7th ed. (Upper Saddle River, NJ: Prentice Hall, 2000), 248–254.

Chapter 5

1. Albert Murray, *Stomping the Blues* (New York: McGraw-Hill, 1976), 126.

2. Alan Morrison, "You Got to Be Original, Man," *Jazz Record*, July 1946. Quoted in Frank Büchmann-Møller, *You Just Fight For Your Life: The Story of Lester Young* (New York: Praeger, 1990), 142.

3. Valerie Wilmer, *Jazz People* (Indianapolis: Bobbs-Merrill, 1970), 123.

4. Ignacio Camargo, quoted in Gilbert Chase, *The Music of Spain*, 2nd ed. (New York: Dover, 1959), 104.

Discography

Hunting down recordings is easier than it used to be, thanks to Internet search engines and music download services. Most recordings identified in the text by artist and date should be easy to locate. Almost every performance cited in the book was available as of fall 2009. The first place to look for early (pre-1935) jazz is the streaming audio site redhotjazz.com. Many early jazz, swing, and bebop recordings are available for streaming at jazz-on-line.com.

Generally, recordings warrant inclusion here only if spotlighted in the text or insufficiently identified there, or if an artist's multiple recordings of the same piece make finding the right performance tricky. The track timings (which may vary slightly from edition to edition) and recording dates will help on that score.

Chapter 1: Basics

Cozy Cole, "Father Co-Operates." February 22, 1944. Master take (4:49) on *Cozy Cole 1944*. Chronological Classics. The full four-take sequence is on *The Complete Coleman Hawkins on Keynote*. Mercury.

Miles Davis, "S'posin'." November 16, 1955 (5:16). He recorded it only once; originally on *Miles*, aka *The New Miles Davis Quintet*. Prestige.

Duke Ellington, "Mood Indigo." Compare October 14, 1930 (Okeh/ Columbia), and October 17, 1930 (Brunswick/Decca)—(both 3:09). Numerous issues.

Dexter Gordon, "Rhythm-a-ning." May 4, 1969 (24:13). On *XXL—Live at the Left Bank*. Prestige.

Coleman Hawkins, "Body and Soul." October 11, 1939 (3:03). RCA. Numerous issues.

Jones-Smith Incorporated (Count Basie), "Boogie Woogie (I May Be Wrong)." November 9, 1936 (3:16). Columbia. Numerous issues.

Charlie Parker, "Parker's Mood." September 18, 1948, master take (3:04). Savoy.

Chapter 2: Origins to 1940

"Down Home Rag." The James Reese Europe, Versatile Four, and Wilbur Sweatman versions are on *Ragtime to Jazz 1 1912–1919*. Timeless Historical.

Count Basie, "One O'Clock Jump." July 7, 1937 (3:03). Decca. Numerous issues.

Duke Ellington, "Black and Tan Fantasy." October 26, 1927 (3:11). Victor/RCA. Numerous issues.

Bud Freeman, "The Eel." October 21 (3:02) and November 17, 1933 (3:22). Both on *Eddie Condon 1927–1938*. Chronological Classics.

Jelly Roll Morton demonstrating the origins and development of "Tiger Rag." May 23, 1938. In Morton, *The Library of Congress Recordings by Alan Lomax.* Rounder, disc 2, tracks 8–10.

Django Reinhardt, with Coleman Hawkins and orchestra, "Avalon." March 2, 1935 (3:05). Numerous issues include *Coleman Hawkins in Europe* (Timeless Historical) and *Django with His American Friends* (DRG).

Chapter 3: 1940–1960

"Bounkam Solo (Burkina Faso)." 1973 (3:55). On the anthology *West Africa: Drum, Chant, and Instrumental Music.* Nonesuch/Explorer.

John Coltrane, "Mr. Day." October 24, 1960 (7:56). On *Coltrane Plays the Blues.* Atlantic.

Duke Ellington, "Cotton Tail" (sometimes spelled as one word). May 4, 1940 (3:16). "Ko-Ko." March 6, 1940 (2:44). Numerous issues. Both on *Never No Lament: The Blanton-Webster Band.* RCA.

Bill Evans, "Peace Piece." December 15, 1958 (6:43). On *Everybody Digs Bill Evans.* Riverside.

Ella Fitzgerald, "How High the Moon." December 20, 1947 (3:16). "Oh, Lady Be Good" (often listed as "Lady Be Good"). March 19, 1947 (3:08). Decca. Numerous issues.

Dizzy Gillespie, "Manteca." December 30, 1947 (3:08). RCA.

———, "Salt Peanuts." May 11, 1945 (3:18). Guild/Savoy.

Lionel Hampton, "Flying Home." May 26, 1942 (3:13). Decca. Numerous issues.

Woody Herman, "Four Brothers." December 27, 1947 (3:17). "Your Father's Mustache." September 5, 1945 (3:22). Both on *Blowin' Up a Storm: The Columbia Years 1945–1947.* Columbia.

Charles Mingus, "Moanin'" and "Wednesday Night Prayer Meeting." February 4, 1959 (8:04 and 5:39). Both on *Blues and Roots.* Atlantic.

————, Charles Mingus, Instrumental dialogues with Eric Dolphy, "What Love." October 20, 1960 (15:24). On *Charles Mingus Presents Charles Mingus*. Candid.

Thelonious Monk, "Trinkle, Tinkle." July 1957 (6:40). On *Thelonious Monk with John Coltrane*. Jazzland/Riverside. Similar issues.

Lee Morgan, "Bess." February 8, 1960 (6:27). On *Here's Lee Morgan*. Vee Jay.

Shorty Rogers and His Giants, "Popo." October 8, 1951 (2:59). Capitol.

Shorty Rogers (quintet), "Martians Go Home." March 1, 1955 (7:57). Atlantic.

Sarah Vaughan, "Lover Man." Two versions: with Dizzy Gillespie, May 11, 1945 (3:25), Guild/Savoy, numerous issues; with her trio, April 2, 1954 (3:18), along with "Shulie a Bop," on *Swingin' Easy*. EmArcy/Universal.

Chapter 4: 1960–1980

Air, "The Ragtime Dance" and "Weeping Willow Rag" (both by Scott Joplin). May 1979 (9:20 and 11:31). On *The Complete Novus and Columbia Recordings of Henry Threadgill and Air*. Mosaic.

Carla Bley, "Ida Lupino." 1976 (7:57). On *Dinner Music*. Watt.

Anthony Braxton. " . . . solo alto, wind trios, two-horn quartets with bass and drums, big band, four symphony orchestras . . . " plus the saxophone quartet, the march "Opus 58," and Scott Joplin's "Maple Leaf Rag" are on *The Complete Arista Recordings of Anthony Braxton*. Mosaic.

Betty Carter, "Sounds (Movin' On)." December 1979 (25:19). On *The Audience with Betty Carter*. Verve.

Ornette Coleman, "Ramblin'." October 9, 1959 (6:38). On *Change of the Century*. Atlantic.

Miles Davis, "Masqualero." May 17, 1967 (8:53). On *Sorcerer*. Columbia.

Keith Jarrett, "American quartet." *The Survivor's Suite*, April 1976. ECM. "European quartet." *My Song*, October 31 and November 1, 1977. ECM.

Steve Lacy (with Enrico Rava, Johnny Dyani and Louis Moholo). *The Forest and the Zoo*. October 8, 1966. ESP.

Cecil Taylor, "Unit Structure/As of Now/Section." May 19, 1966 (17:48). On *Unit Structures*. Blue Note.

Chapter 5: After 1980

John Carter (octet), *Dauwhe* (first volume in his *Roots and Folklore* series). 1982. Black Saint.

Steve Coleman, "Wights Waits for Weights." March 1985 (5:14). Available for free (as is much of Coleman's music) at his Web site: http://www.m-base.com/download.html#motherland.

Wynton Marsalis, "Hustle Bustle." July 27 or 28, 1992 (4:36). On *Citi Movement*. Columbia.

Misha Mengelberg and the ICP Orchestra (with Steve Lacy). *Two Programs: Herbie Nichols—Thelonious Monk*. 1984, 1986. ICP.

Paul Motian, Bill Frisell, and Joe Lovano. *I Have the Room above Her*. April 2004. ECM.

David Murray, "Flowers for Albert." July 1982 (9:42). On David Murray Octet, *Murray's Steps*. Black Saint.

Henry Threadgill Sextett. "Spotted Dick Is Pudding." September 20, 1987 (9:00). On *The Complete Novus and Columbia Recordings of Henry Threadgill and Air*. Mosaic.

Suggestions for Further Reading

General Reference and Chapter 1: Basics

Gioia, Ted. *The History of Jazz*. 2nd ed. New York: Oxford University Press, 2011.

Hentoff, Nat, and Nat Shapiro. *Hear Me Talkin' to Ya: An Oral History of Jazz*. New York: Dover, 1966.

Kernfeld, Barry, ed. *The New Grove Dictionary of Jazz*. 2nd ed. 3 vols. New York: Grove Dictionaries / London: Macmillan, 2002.

Chapter 2: Origins to 1940

Basie, Count, with Albert Murray. *Good Morning Blues: The Autobiography of Count Basie*. New York: Random House, 1985.

Bergreen, Laurence. *Louis Armstrong: An Extravagant Life*. New York: Broadway Books, 1997.

Brooks, Tim. *Lost Sounds: Blacks and the Birth of the Recording Industry, 1890–1919*. Urbana and Chicago: University of Illinois Press, 2004.

Chilton, John. *The Song of the Hawk: The Life and Recordings of Coleman Hawkins*. Ann Arbor: University of Michigan Press, 1990.

Dahl, Linda. *Morning Glory: A Biography of Mary Lou Williams*. New York: Pantheon, 1999.

―――. *Stormy Weather: The Music and Lives of a Century of Jazzwomen*. New York: Pantheon, 1984.

Daniels, Douglas Henry. *Lester Leaps In: The Life and Times of Lester "Pres" Young*. Boston: Beacon, 2002.

Giddins, Gary. *Satchmo*. New York: Doubleday, 1988.

Gushee, Lawrence. *Pioneers of Jazz: The Story of the Creole Band*. New York: Oxford, 2005.

Hasse, John Edward, ed. *Ragtime: Its History, Composers and Music*. New York: Schirmer, 1985.

Russell, Ross. *Jazz Style in Kansas City and the Southwest*. 1973. Reprint, Berkeley: University of California Press, 1983.

Schuller, Gunther. *Early Jazz: Its Roots and Musical Development*. New York: Oxford University Press, 1968.

―――. *The Swing Era: The Development of Jazz 1930–1945*. New York: Oxford University Press, 1989.

Shipton, Alyn. *Fats Waller: The Cheerful Little Earful*. Rev. ed. New York: Continuum, 2002.

Stewart, Rex. *Jazz Masters of the '30s*. New York: Macmillan, 1972.

Sublette, Ned. *Cuba and Its Music: From the First Drums to the Mambo*. Chicago: Chicago Review Press, 2004.

Tucker, Mark, ed. *The Duke Ellington Reader*. New York: Oxford University Press, 1993.

Whitehead, Kevin. "Jazz Worldwide." In *Jazz: The First Century*, ed. John Edward Hasse (New York, William Morrow, 2000), 169–193.

Chapter 3: 1940–1960

Chambers, Jack. *Milestones: The Music and Times of Miles Davis*. Originally published in two volumes, 1983, 1985. Reprint, New York: Da Capo, 1998.

Condon, Eddie, with Thomas Sugrue. *We Called It Music*. Rev. ed., 1962. Reprint, New York: Da Capo, 1992.

Dance, Stanley. *The World of Duke Ellington*. New York: Scribner's, 1970.

Davis, Francis. "*Kind of Blue* at 50." Essay included in Miles Davis, *Kind of Blue: Legacy Edition*. New York: Columbia Records, 2009.

DeVeaux, Scott. *The Birth of Bebop: A Social and Musical History*. Berkeley: University of California Press, 1997.

Gillespie, Dizzy, and Al Fraser. *To Be or Not . . . to Bop*. Garden City, NY: Doubleday, 1979.

Gioia, Ted. *West Coast Jazz: Modern Jazz in California, 1945–1960*. New York: Oxford University Press, 1992.

Nisenson, Eric. *Open Sky: Sonny Rollins and His World of Improvisation*. New York: Da Capo, 2000.

Priestley, Brian. *Chasin' the Bird: The Life and Legacy of Charlie Parker*. Rev. ed. New York: Oxford University Press, 2006.

Rattenbury, Ken. *Duke Ellington: Jazz Composer*. New Haven, CT: Yale University Press, 1990.

Rosenthal, David H. *Hard Bop: Jazz and Black Music, 1955–1965*. New York: Oxford University Press, 1992.

Santoro, Gene. *Myself When I Am Real: The Life and Music of Charles Mingus*. New York: Oxford University Press, 2000.

Tucker, Sherrie. *Swing Shift: "All-Girl" Bands of the 1940s*. Durham, NC: Duke University Press, 2000.

Van der Bliek, Rob, ed. *The Thelonious Monk Reader*. New York: Oxford University Press, 2001.

Chapter 4: 1960–1980

Bauer, William R. *Open the Door: The Life and Music of Betty Carter*. Ann Arbor: University of Michigan Press, 2002.

Belden, Bob. "Annotations." Essay included in CD box set *Miles Davis Quintet: 1965–'68*. New York: Columbia Records, 1998.

Gridley, Mark. *Jazz Styles: History and Analysis*. 7th ed. Upper Saddle River, NJ: Prentice Hall, 2000.

Jost, Ekkehard. *Free Jazz*. 1974. Reprint, New York: Da Capo, 1994.

Lewis, George E. *A Power Stronger Than Itself: The AACM and American Experimental Music*. Chicago: University of Chicago Press, 2008.

Litweiler, John. *The Freedom Principle: Jazz after 1958*. New York: William Morrow, 1984.

Nicholson, Stuart. *Jazz Rock: A History*. New York: Schirmer, 1998.

Ratliff, Ben. *Coltrane: The Story of a Sound*. New York: Farrar, Straus and Giroux, 2007.

Spellman, A. B. *Four Lives in the Be-bop Business*. New York: Pantheon, 1966.

Szwed, John F. *Space Is the Place: The Lives and Times of Sun Ra*. New York: Pantheon, 1997.

Taylor, Arthur. *Notes and Tones: Musician-to-Musician Interviews*. Rev. ed. New York: Da Capo, 1993.

Whitehead, Kevin. *New Dutch Swing*. New York: Billboard, 1998.

Wilmer, Valerie. *As Serious as Your Life: The Story of the New Jazz*. London: Allison & Busby, 1977.

Chapter 5: After 1980

Davis, Francis. *In the Moment: Jazz in the 1980s*. New York: Oxford University Press, 1986.

Gourse, Leslie. *Madame Jazz: Contemporary Women Instrumentalists.* New York: Oxford University Press, 1995.

Hamilton, Andy. *Lee Konitz: Conversations on the Improviser's Art.* Ann Arbor: University of Michigan Press, 2007.

Lock, Graham. *Forces in Motion: Anthony Braxton and the Meta-Reality of Improvised Music.* London: Quartet, 1988.

Mandel, Howard. *Future Jazz.* New York: Oxford University Press, 1999.

Murray, Albert. *Stomping the Blues.* New York: McGraw-Hill, 1976.

Porter, Eric. *What Is This Thing Called Jazz? African American Musicians as Artists, Critics, and Activists.* Berkeley: University of California Press, 2002.

Santoro, Gene. *Dancing in Your Head: Jazz, Blues, Rock, and Beyond.* New York: Oxford University Press, 1994.

Szwed, John F. *So What: The Life of Miles Davis.* New York: Simon & Schuster, 2002.

Index

Note: Page numbers followed by "*f*" refer to figures.